Once the hinge of democracy, the media no
news'—Winter's analysis is strong.
—*Globe and Mail*

Democracy's Oxygen is an important book: it enhances the political discourse on a critical subject and refutes the view that those concerned with corporate control of the news are wacky conspiracy seekers. Clearly, one doesn't have to believe in any kind of grand conspiracy to see why ownership of the news media by a handful of people can't be good for democracy.
—*Literary Review of Canada*

Winter's book is an invaluable reference tool. Its research is particularly strong in the profiles of Black, his fellow baron Paul Desmarais, and the publishing giant Québecor.
—*Quill & Quire*

In the increasingly stifling atmosphere of Canadian democracy, Winter's book is a breath of fresh air. Winter—admirably—writes in direct and accessible language.
—*Canadian Dimension*

Democracy's Oxygen, by media critic James Winter, is a timely release. Winter's main point that the left needs to develop and vastly expand its own media is undeniable.
—*Briarpatch*

One of the best things about Winter's work is that it stands outside the loop, where the flatness of the media landscape isn't so evident.
—*Now Magazine*

A valuable resource. Winter presents a well-documented case that Black had a definite political agenda, and his acquisition of newspapers the world over was a conscious grab for political power.
—*Hour Magazine*

James Winter has hit on a hot topic. Contains truths which only those in an advanced state of denial could ignore.
—*Ottawa Citizen*

James Winter's investigation is about nothing less than the corporate takeover of public expression. Read it.
—*Maude Barlow, Council for Canadians*

Media THINK

Media THINK

James Winter

Montréal/New York/London

Black Rose Books No. EE306
Hardcover ISBN: 1-55164-055-4 (bound)
Paperback ISBN: 1-55164-054-6 (pbk.)

Canadian Cataloguing in Publication Data
Winter, James P. (James Patrick), 1952-
MediaThink

Includes bibliographical references.
Hardcover ISBN: 1-55164-055-4 (bound)
Paperback ISBN: 1-55164-054-6 (pbk.)

1. Mass media and public opinion. 2. Mass media--Political aspects.
3. Mass media--Social aspects. I. Title

P91.W56 2000   302.23   C00-900455-6

Cover design by Associés libres, Montréal

C.P. 1258	2250 Military Road	99 Wallis Road
Succ. Place du Parc	Tonawanda, NY	London, E9 5LN
Montréal, H2W 2R3	14150	England
Canada	USA	UK

To order books:

In Canada: (phone) 1-800-565-9523 (fax) 1-800-221-9985
email: utpbooks@utpress.utoronto.ca

In United States: (phone) 1-800-283-3572 (fax) 1-651-917-6406

In the UK & Europe: (phone) London 44 (0)20 8986-4854 (fax) 44 (0)20 8533-5821
email: order@centralbooks.com

Our Web Site address: http://www.web.net/blackrosebooks

A publication of the Institute of Policy Alternatives of Montréal (IPAM)

Printed in Canada

The Canada Council   Le Conseil des Arts
for the Arts   du Canada

CONTENTS

to the heroic people of East Timor

PREFACE

As the page proofs for this book were being prepared, two hijacked planes destroyed the World Trade Centre in New York, while another crashed into the Pentagon in Washington. Mainstream news coverage of the so-called "Attack on America" provided a classic example of the MediaThink phenomenon detailed in this book. Everywhere, Canadian news media emulated their American cousins, competing to be the best allies for the global policies of U.S. President George W. Bush.

Because of the grave consequences and ramifications of war, when one appears imminent it is the role of the news media to hold governments accountable to a considerable burden of proof. Possibly moreso than at any other time, this is when news media must perform their much-vaunted "watchdog" function over governments. The press and the airwaves should be filled with questioning, challenges, and diverse viewpoints. In the public interest, no effort should be spared with respect to a full exploration of justifications and alternatives. This is if the media are to serve the public interest. If instead, they serve other interests, then things will be different.

In the aftermath of September 11, so uniform was the media perspective that it hardly matters which corporation you study. *The Windsor Star*, for example, carried barely a single critical word of objection (except for an occasional letter) versus literally hundreds of pages filled with faithful columnists, editorials and news stories championing the cause of war. The Montreal *Gazette* refused to run a mildly critical piece by regular columnist Lyle Stewart, who said in an email that it was cut "for reasons I don't completely understand."

The Globe and Mail carried a huge, 72-point headline the day after September 11, calling it "A Day of Infamy," using Franklin Delano Roosevelt's words about Pearl Harbour and indicating this was an act of war. The media drum beating saw them adopt a uniform logo ("Attack on America") and subsequent bellicose themes such as "America Fights Back," "America's New War," then "Operation Infinite Justice," and finally "Operation Enduring Freedom,"much as they did in the Gulf War with "Operation Desert Storm." With the other topics in this book I have intentionally delayed my analysis for at least one or two years, to augment the potential for greater perspective. The publisher and I felt that owing to the importance of these latest events, some instant analysis is in order. An examination of the ways in which the media justified the policies of the U.S. Administration, is instructive. I will discuss these under six categories, beginning with:

WORLD WAR III

The media response was sensational, emotional, and repetitive, soon lapsing into persistent warmongering, clamouring for vengeance. Eventually, a few commentators called for calm and a measured response: but most wanted blood. The same national security apparatus which couldn't detect anything coming, could, within just a few hours, identify Osama bin Laden as the culprit. Within a week, George Bush was demanding bin Laden's head, as "Wanted Dead or Alive." It was the return of the wild west. Soon, he would be heading up a posse of high tech vigilantes, with a national lynching on the horizon and nary a courtroom in sight.

Lorne Gunter of Southam wrote that "retaliatory measures should be brutal against those directly involved, as well as against those, like, for example, the Afghan government if bid Laden is responsible."[1] Marcus Gee of *The Globe and Mail* wrote that the U.S. wrath would "shake the world."

"Expect an all-out war on terrorism that will almost certainly include some kind of U.S. military strike. Expect a far more assertive United States, far more willing to throw its weight around and far less likely to listen to the doubts of its allies on the United Nations,"[2] Gee wrote. The way they listened to UN doubts over Kosovo, for instance. Peter Worthington of *The Toronto Sun* attacked George Bush's weak-kneed response. "Except for one line, George Bush was more grief counsellor than warrior leader...Americans want to fight back. So should we all...Damn caution. Fight back!"[3] A column by Richard Gwyn of the *Toronto Star* was headlined, "Expect Americans to launch powerful anti-terrorist war."[4] A *Toronto Star* editorial the day after referred to "an unparalleled act of barbarism that Americans took as an act of war."

And the enemy was built up, just as Saddam Hussein's "battle-hardened Elite Republican Guard" was built up before the Gulf War. *Toronto Star* columnist Stephen Handelman wrote September 12, "[the] U.S. administration will have to mobilize effectively for war against an enemy that has proved himself as well-organized and as efficient as any this country has seen before."

The media indicated that this calculated atrocity could only have been carried out by one man: Osama bin Laden. Within just a few hours they had zeroed in on him, and were running photos and accounts of his alleged terrorism. The analogies to the Japanese attack on Pearl Harbour, which drew the U.S. into World War II, were rampant. While *The Globe and Mail* headline read, "A Day of Infamy," *The Toronto Star* reprinted FDR's entire speech to Congress after Pearl Harbour. Within the week, Defence Minister Art Eggleton was quoted as saying, "I think [Canada is] going to play a major role, a frontline role" in any military strike against terrorism.[5] Later, as Jean Chretien scurried down to Washington to confer with Bush, columnist Gord Henderson complained bitterly that Bush didn't solicit Canadian military aid.[6] With "one of the world's most illustrious military legacies," Henderson lamented, Canada has been "reduced by decades of government negligence" to just a "helpless bystander" during the "first great showdown between good and evil in the 21st century."

The presumption had been that any war would include Canada, of course. Graham Greene, an editor at *The Ottawa Citizen*, wrote, "the United States needs to know that its allies will stand with it, including militarily, if its retaliatory actions provoke a wider conflict."[7] *The Globe and Mail* editorialized that "Prime Minister Jean Chrétien should establish a 'war cabinet' of senior ministers and officials."[8]

The U.S. media were even more warlike. *USA Today* declared an "Act of War," while *The New York Times* proclaimed "World War III." And, it wasn't just a headline. Thomas Friedman asked in *The Times*, "Does my country really understand that this is World War III?" Detroit TV news anchor Carmen Harlan commented, "If this isn't war, I don't know what war is."[9] Within two days, *The Washington Times* decided it was "Time To Use The Nuclear Option." U.S. Deputy Secretary of Defense Paul Wolfowitz, spoke of "ending states who sponsor terrorism." R.W. Apple, Jr., wrote in *The Washington Post*, "In this new kind [of] war...there are no neutral states or geographical confines. Us or them. You are either with us or against us."[10] The analysts and commentators in the media bounced back and forth with the Pentagon, State Department and White House officials, exchanging and intensifying their hyperbole and rhetoric.

In *The Philadelphia Inquirer*, David Perlmutter demonstrated an understanding of recent historical events in Iraq, Bosnia, and Kosovo. He warned that if states allegedly harbouring terrorists do not do Washington's bidding, they must: "Prepare for the systematic destruction of every power plant, every oil refinery, every pipeline, every military base, every government office in the entire country...the complete collapse of their economy and government for a generation."

In other words, it will be similar to what they did in Iraq, and Kosovo. As Fairness and Accuracy in Reporting (FAIR) indicated, American media advocated pursuing civilian targets, contrary to the Geneva Conventions. Columnist Ann Coulter wrote in *The New York Daily News*, for example, that:

> This is no time to be precious about locating the exact individuals directly involved in this particular terrorist attack...*We should invade their countries, kill their leaders and convert them to Christianity*. We weren't punctilious about locating and punishing only Hitler and his

top officers. We carpet-bombed German cities; we killed civilians. That's war. And this is war.[11]

Over at *The Washington Times*, guest columnist Thomas Woodrow was arguing that it's "Time to Use the Nuclear Option," as to do less would be seen "as cowardice."[12]

In their thirst for vengeance and war, the media ignored or dispensed with international law. Gone were international boundaries, and the presumption of innocence until guilt is proven in a court of law. After a century of fuelling wars and coups, death and destruction abroad, a single attack on the domestic U.S. was enough to see this allegedly 'civilized, free and democratic' country revert to the crude motto of: an eye for an eye.

WE ARE THE WORLD

The World War III which they anticipated was justified, according to the mainstream media, because what took place was not just an attack on three buildings in two American cities, but on the world itself. This is because the U.S. is not simply another country: it represents freedom, democracy, and civilization itself. *The Windsor Star* editorialized that,

> The real targets of the hijackers and their flying bombs were freedom, democracy, and capitalism...It is time to draw a line in the sand. On one side lies democracy, individual freedom, and the capitalism that makes the two most essential qualities of life possible. On the other side lies terrorism.[13]

The Toronto Star said "The assault on America is a threat to every civilized nation."[14] Lorne Gunter of Southam wrote that "Nothing less than the western way of life is at stake."[15] Graham Greene of *The Ottawa Citizen* said, "this was not just an attack on American targets or U.S. citizens. It was a well-planned and deliberate attack on the very essence of all truly democratic countries."[16] Playing the following week in his first game as a New York Ranger, the NHL's Eric Lindros told CNN, "We're all in this together. It affects all of us."

IT HAPPENED FOR NO REASON

In the mainstream media universe, whatever revenge would be taken was all the more justified because this was more than an act of violence: it was a senseless act of wanton destruction, gigantic in proportion. So, even though it was termed "an act of war," like Pearl Harbour, it was an unprovoked attack which precipitated the war that would follow. The response to it would be an act of war, but not the terrorism itself, which if it was, would lend it legitimacy. In fact, it was a criminal act, for which the appropriate response was legal rather than militaristic.

There are no reasons because these people are fanatics. Paul Rosen, an invited guest on CBC radio's *Ontario Today* call-in program asked in response to a question about potential negotiations, "Can you reason with the Devil?"

To the media, like the U.S. administration, there was no precipitating act. It was unimaginable that there was any discontent with U.S. foreign policy. It was impossible that such a tragedy could be backlash for (nonexistent) U.S. aggression or economic exploitation. For example, Richard Gwyn wrote in *the Toronto Star* that, "It was done without warning, not in response to American aggression but as an act of aggression in itself." Editorially, The 'liberal' and relatively 'progressive' *Toronto Star* said that it's not even possible to imagine any justification. "Prime Minister Jean Chretien has rightly denounced this 'cowardly and depraved assault,' for which there can be no imaginable justification."[17]

Margaret Wente, former managing editor of the *Globe and Mail*, wrote, within 24 hours of the attack:

> Those who are responsible are most likely men from remote desert lands. Men from ancient tribal cultures built on blood and revenge. Men whose unshakable beliefs and implacable hatreds go back many centuries farther than the United States and its young ideas of democracy, pluralism, and freedom...Men capable...of giving up their lives for the greater glory of Allah...Men...with the implacable determination of fanatics.[18]

The Globe and Mail editorialized, "This is a show of power and strength. It is a show of cold-hearted brutality perpetrated by fanatics who have discarded all pretense of humanity or morality." What's more, even if they did have "a foreign political cause, their campaign has now lost all international support and legitimacy."[19]

A *Globe* reporter in Calgary, Dawn Walton, wrote that her husband explained to their young daughter that "some bad guys...just wanted to hurt people" and that's why they crashed into the WTC.[20]

"Obviously [Osama bin Laden] is filled with hate for the United States and for everything we stand for...freedom and democracy," U.S. Vice President Dick Cheney told Tim Russert on *Meet The Press*, September 16. He went on, "It must have something to do with his background, his own upbringing." Or perhaps it was the support he received from the CIA during Afghanistan's struggle with the Soviet Union. According to the media, terrorists are merely a product of their own personal insanity. They are not seen in a global context where there are deep divisions between rich and poor; where wealth and power are concentrated in the hands of a few. Oblivious to these conditions and the true nature of U.S. interventions abroad, they can offer us no explanations.

Hence, as with Montreal Massacrist Marc Lepine, who murdered 14 women in 1989, it was an act devoid of anything other than personal context. Lepine was portrayed as a madman, rather than as being influenced by our anti-feminist culture.

ATTACK ON CANADIAN IMMIGRATION POLICY

The media renewed their ongoing campaign to get the federal government to tighten up on immigration policy. (See Chapter Five.) Columnist Gord Henderson of *The Windsor Star* lambasted "Those weak-kneed decision-makers in the Liberal government and federal bureaucracy who let Canada become a patsy for potential mass murderers from around the globe."[21] Stewart Bell of *The National Post* said, "Through negligence and indifference, the Canadian government has permitted virtually every major terrorist organization to operate within its borders." Bell wrote that "Canada's vulnerability to infiltration by terrorists is deeply entrenched. Its refugee laws are probably the most lax in the Western world."[22]

Editorially, *The Post* said "Canada has been a porous staging area and conduit for terrorist conspiracies in the past. The Canadian government should not wait till U.S. authorities complete their investigation. They need to reform our immigration, refugee and visitor entry procedures now."[23] In its editorial, *The Globe and Mail* said that although the federal government just finished overhauling Canada's immigration rules three months earlier, and they were still before the Senate, they "should review the issue again with particular focus on the new war on terrorism."[24] The Senate was pressured to compact five weeks of debate on the news legislation into just four days. *The Toronto Star* quoted Jean Chretien, to the effect that "Perhaps there will be a need of changing some of the [immigration] legislations."[25]

REINFORCING RACISM

Media coverage was rooted in nationalism, patriotism, jingoism, but also racism. About 7000 predominantly middle and upper middle class, mostly White American lives are "worth" much more attention, grieving, and retaliation, than the 700,000 Iraqis who died during and since the Gulf War, or the 300,000 East Timorese who died since the Indonesian invasion of 1975, et cetera. Given the ease with which this information may be had, the media are willfully blind to these deaths.

In a revealing comment, a psychiatrist told *The Windsor Star*, "The people of America will now live with what the people of Israel have lived with for generations." No mention of the far greater tribulations the Palestinians have endured: they remain off the radar screen.[26] The coverage has not simply been racist: there are elements of classism and xenophobia, as well. And although some people from around the world were in the World Trade Centre, and died, this event was significant not due to them but because it was an "Attack on America," and specifically on the monied, heartland of New York.

The racist coverage, lack of context, and other elements contributed to the backlash in which a Sikh Indian was murdered in Texas. *The Windsor Star* ran a wire service story which began, "Those who look like Muslims—but aren't—say they are suffering from angry fellow Americans."[27] But how do you look like a Muslim? What does someone who is Roman Catholic look like?

A DIVERSIONARY TACTIC

The glut of media coverage diverted attention away from the real "Attack on America," the attack on the working class and poor through elite policies which favour the rich. This takes the form of tax breaks, cuts to welfare, social programs, health and public education. "Right to work" laws are an attack on people, eliminating minimum wages, as are free trade policies which continually transfer jobs to the cheapest available labour market. There is also excessive corporate and individual profiteering. These policies have led to an increasing gap between the rich and poor.

The Attack coverage has rallied Americans and others to the cause, and led to a climate of emotional hysteria. In this atmosphere there is even less national and international monitoring of U.S. activities abroad. The U.S. Administration has capitalized on this hysteria to win funding and approval from Congress, and advance support around the world permitting forthcoming repressive and brutal acts which, like their antecedent actions, will far outweigh the effects of the hijackings. At this writing, the Taliban government in Afghanistan has asked Osama bin Laden to leave that country, within a reasonable time period. They subsequently offered to turn him over to the U.S., in exchange for proof of his involvement in the September 11 attacks. But this response to the U.S. threats was juxtaposed against the irrepressible American war machine, which was already converging on Afghanistan, named "Operation Enduring Freedom" by the Pentagon, funded and approved by Congress, and condoned by ostensibly peace loving nations around the world. The response of the Bush administration was that they would "not negotiate" with the Taliban. They would not even provide the Taliban with the same evidence reportedly given to NATO, and other countries such as Canada.[28]

PROMOTING U.S. POLICIES

As evidenced by their early coverage of the "Attack on America," the media not only report on, but seldom stray from, the policies, statements and spin of the U.S. Administration and its client governments in Canada, Britain, and elsewhere. This may mean simply overlooking some things, or suffering from apparent historical amnesia, or adhering to what George Orwell called the "prevailing orthodoxy." This is what I have chosen to call "MediaThink." The consequences may lead, as in the current case, to amplification of the terror, horror and deaths. Rather than abetting U.S. geopolitics, in response to the attack on the World Trade Centre the media might have chosen to demand that the U.S. cease and desist from the bloody international interventions it has perpetrated over the last century, from Cuba to the Philippines, from Guatamala to Kosovo.[29] Were the U.S. Administration to agree, I suspect that the violence would greatly diminish, along with the "blowback" terrorism (to use the CIA term) inflicted in response. Obviously, as the mainstream media are a crucial component of a global agenda which involves the U.S. Administration, transglobal corporations, the World Bank, International Monetary Fund, and others, it would be heretical, 'suicidal' and perhaps patricidal for them to attack, criticize, or even differ with stated policy.

As with Orwell's Winston Smith in *1984*, severe penalties are in store for the foolish few who dare to stray from the one true view of the world handed down by our leaders. For example, Bill Maher, host of the TV programme *Politically Incorrect* wandered out onto thin ice when he ventured that, whatever you might think of the terrorists their actions were not "cowardly," as labelled by Bush and Co., compared with dropping bombs on civilians from great heights. Federal Express, and Sears Roebuck and Co. pulled their ads from Maher's programme, after indicating there were consumer complaints.

This censorship, trouncing of civil liberties and suppression of dissent, is nothing new. During the Gulf War, for example, at a war protest rally held at the SUNY college campus in New Paltz N.Y., professor Barbara Scott urged American military personnel not to kill innocent people. In the enormous brouhaha following the event, the media dubbed her "Baghdad Barbara," in reference to Tokyo Rose of WW2. Republican Senator Charles Cook went so far as to publicly accuse Scott of treason. Letter campaigns were aimed at the college president and then-Governor Mario Cuomo, urging them to fire Scott. Meanwhile, hate mail arrived at her office.[30]

In Canada, on October 1, 2001, University of British Columbia professor Sunera Thobani spoke out at a conference on violence against women, held in Ottawa. Dr. Thobani said the U.S. is "the most dangerous and most powerful global force unleashing horrific levels of violence." Although she empathized with the suffering caused by the September 11 attacks, she asked, "do we feel any pain for the victims of U.S. aggression?" The 500 women in the audience interrupted Thobani's speech with cheers and a standing ovation. But the media lapdogs leapt to the attack on this "feminist," and "former president of the National Action Committee on the Status of Women," condemning what they described as a "hateful, manipulative and outrageous rant."[31]

The National Post reached out to Gordon Campbell, premier of B.C., for his characterization of her remarks as "hateful, destructive and very disturbing," along with Alliance leader Stockwell Day and Gwen Landolt of Real Women of Canada, a reactionary women's group. Columnists such as Christie Blatchford and Claire Hoy attacked Thobani as "vicious" and "hate-filled" and a "bitter bit," and her audience as "collected wing-nuts." Because the conference received government funding, Stockwell Day said it was "unacceptable" for Thobani "to be saying the things that she did...at taxpayers' expense." He called for prime minister Chretien to inform the U.S. government that Canada repudiates Thobani's message.

Of course, there was no hatred in Thobani's talk, merely a call for peace and compassion for all victims.

In contrast to the corporate media hysteria, as did Sunera Thobani, the alternative media placed the terrorist attacks in the historical context of U.S. "interventions" abroad and aggression. While not excusing the terrorists, and also mourning the 7000 civilian lives taken, through the writings of Michael Albert and Noam Chomsky and others, Zmagazine, Indymedia, etc., provided information which was crucial for understanding the events. In "Five Reasons Not to Go to War," for example, Michael Albert and Stephen R. Shalom argued that war would be horribly wrong for at least five reasons: 1. Guilt hasn't yet been proven; 2. War would violate International Law; 3. War would be unlikely to eliminate those responsible for the September 11 attacks; 4. Huge numbers of innocent people will die; 5. War will reduce the security of U.S. citizens.[32]

In sum, as indicated earlier, at times such as this it is the media's responsibility to hold governments accountable for their decision to go to war, to defend the public interest by providing intense scrutiny, demanding evidence and reasons, and displaying a wide range of diverse perspectives. This is a time for the adversarial journalism of the fourth estate: for watchdogs rather than lapdogs. Instead, the corporate media resorted to frenzied advocacy of an illegal vigilante war, promoting violence, hatred and blindness to reason. They have functioned, with few exceptions, as an extension of the U.S. administration, demanding a violent, vengeful and bloody war.

NOTES

1. Lorne Gunter, "Retaliation is a must," *The Windsor Star*, September 13, 2001.

2. Marcus Gee, "The sleeping giant wakes up angry," *The Globe and Mail*, September 12, 2001.

3. Peter Worthington, "America Needs a Leader," *Toronto Sun*, September 13, 2001, A7.

4. Richard Gwyn, "Expect Americans to launch powerful anti-terrorist war," *The Toronto Star*, September 12, 2001, A1.

5. Quoted in Janice Tibbetts, "What can Armed Forces contribute?" *The Windsor Star*, September 18, 2001.

6. Gord Henderson, "Canada as bystander," *The Windsor Star*, September 25, 2001.

7. Graham Greene, "Time to stand with U.S.," *The Windsor Star*, September 12, 2001, A7.

8. Editorial, "It's time to consider how best we can help," *Globe and Mail*, September 18, 2001.

9. Quoted in Ted Shaw, "TV brings terrorism home," *The Windsor Star*, September 12, 2001, A10.

10. These U.S. headlines and quotations are taken from, Jared Israel, Rick Rozoff & Nico Varkevisser, "Washington Wants Afghanistan," www.emperors-clothes.com, September 18, 2001.

11. Ann Coulter, *New York Daily News*, September 12, 2001, quoted in FAIR, Media March to War, September 17, 2001.

12. Quoted in "Media Pundits Advocate Civilian Targets," FAIR, September 24, 2001.

13. Editorial, "Freedom: A struggle that involves us," *The Windsor Star*, September 13, 2001.

14. Editorial, "Democracy will prevail over barbarous hate," *The Toronto Star*, September 12, A26.

15. Lorne Gunter, "Retaliation is a must," *The Windsor Star*, September 13, 2001.

16. Graham Greene, "Time to stand with U.S.," *The Windsor Star*, September 12, A7.

17. Editorial, "Democracy will prevail over barbarous hate," *The Toronto Star*, September 12, A26.

18. Margaret Wente, "U.S. will never be the same." *The Globe and Mail*, September 12, 2001, A1.

19. Editorial, "Let loose the war on global terrorism," *The Globe and Mail*, September 12, 2001, A18.

20. Dawn Walton, "Explaining the day the bogeyman came," *The Globe and Mail*, September 12, 2001, A30.

21. Gord Henderson, "Shameful Times," *The Windsor Star*, September 13, 2001.

22. Stewart Bell, "A conduit for terrorists," *The National Post*, September 13, 2001.

23. Ibid.

24. Editorial, "It's time to consider how best we can help," *The Globe and Mail*, September 18, 2001.

25. CP, "Bush summons PM to White House council," *The Toronto Star*, September 18, 2001.

26. Quoted in Don Lajoie, "Trauma to be felt for years, doc says," *The Windsor Star*, September 12, 2001.

27. Thomas Hargrove, "Backlash hits non-Arab minorities," *The Windsor Star*, September 18, 2001, A8.

28. In the article "Canada Convinced," *The Windsor Star*, October 3, 2001, the newspaper quoted prime minister Jean Chretien as saying that he was convinced of Osama bin Laden's guilt, based upon the secret information provided to him by the Bush administration.

29. For a brief overview, since World War II, see William Blum, "A Brief History of U.S. Interventions: 1945 to the Present," Z magazine, June 1999.

30. For more details, see James Winter, "Truth as the First Casualty," in *Common Cents: Media Portrayal of the Gulf War and Other Events*, Black Rose Books, Montreal, 1992.

31. Mark Hume and Mary Vallis, "Thobani 'rant' called hateful," *The National Post*, October 3, 2001.

32. Michael Albert and Stephen R. Shalom, "Five Reasons Not to Go to War," www.Zmag.org, September 21, 2001.

ACKNOWLEDGMENTS

A number of people graciously helped to improve earlier drafts of the chapters in this book. Sarah Atkinson, Shawn Hupka, Kerry Pither, K.J. Winter and Dr. Vito Signorile read individual chapters and provided suggestions and comments. Dr. Walter Dorn and Dr. Barry Lituchy made invaluable contributions to the chapters on East Timor and Kosovo, respectively. Dave Hall's careful reading and criticisms are gratefully acknowledged. Computer Sam kept the technology tuned. Ann Gallant and Sandy VanZetten provided solid secretarial assistance. Elizabeth Graham and Lisa Soydanbay provided some research assistance, early in the project. Thanks to Linda Barton and Dimitri Roussopoulos at Black Rose Books. Any errors which remain are my own.

Thanks also to my friends and colleagues: Dr. Valerie Scatamburlo-D'Annibale, Dr. Irv Goldman, Dr. Robert Babe, and Dr. Myles Ruggles. Thanks to my children Kaeleigh and Kieran for allowing me to share in your *joie de vivre*, which is as boundless as it is uplifting. And finally, to my favourite ex-journalist, Gail, who read, corrected, talked, listened, tolerated, and above all inspired.

INTRODUCTION

SOME LIES TO EXPOSE

"My starting point is always a feeling of partisanship, a sense of injustice. When I sit down to write a book, I do not say to myself, 'I am going to produce a work of art.' I write it because there is some lie that I want to expose, some fact to which I want to draw attention, and my initial concern is to get a hearing." —George Orwell

In the 1940s British author and journalist Eric Arthur Blair wrote a book of fiction titled *1984*, in which he warned that if citizens were not vigilant the State could come to control our actions, and possibly even our thinking. Blair, who wrote under the pseudonym of George Orwell, produced a book which, like Adam Smith's *Wealth of Nations* before it, became a bible for those who claimed to deplore government intervention of all sorts: from the free marketers to libertarians to cold war warriors, and even, lately, the U.S. National Rifle Association. In the intervening half century these forces have been vigilant, keeping both eyes on Big Brother, ensuring that governments don't grow too strong and beating them back at every turn, all the while championing what they see as the contradictory notions of individualism and personal freedom.

But as with Adam Smith, Orwell's work was oversimplified, misinterpreted, and used for selfish political purposes. For example, suppose that

George Orwell was actually a socialist. Of course, this notion doesn't make 'sense,' because it is beyond the boundaries of *MediaThink*, but in fact it is quite true. Here is what Orwell wrote about the matter in 1947: "Every line of serious work that I have written since 1936 has been written, directly or indirectly, against totalitarianism and for democratic socialism, as I understand it."[1] This doesn't make 'sense' because Orwell is the champion of those mentioned above, who oppose government intervention in the economy: the rabid anti-communists who have equated socialism with communism and communism with totalitarianism.[2] Their goal has been the distortion of socialism and communism and identifying both with the real and imagined horrors in the former Soviet Union, which was neither. Hence, if Orwell is a socialist, then he becomes the very thing he is famous for ridiculing and satirizing in *1984*, and in *Animal Farm*, and elsewhere. That's why it doesn't make 'sense' that Orwell was a socialist, although in fact he was. In the contemporary U.S., socialists and even liberals are now lumped together with 'communists,' truncating the ideological spectrum and political debate itself.

The reason for doing this is simple: it reduces matters to the Manichaean, 'black and white' terms which are an essential element of propaganda and manipulation. If liberalism and its alleged bedmates are 'bad,' then capitalism, democracy and neo-conservatism, which are also equated, and are the only alternative, must be 'good.' In the days of the Cold War, this could simply be represented as a choice between the Russian bear and the American eagle, as repression versus freedom, or by the popular catch phrase: "better dead than red."

In the meantime, another work by Orwell has gone largely unmentioned. In fact, it was the preface Orwell wrote to *Animal Farm*, which was excised from the original publication and only surfaced later with his original manuscript. Rather than writing about totalitarianism in Russia, in his preface Orwell was writing about voluntary literary censorship in Britain at the time, a topic which was much less fashionable.[3] Orwell noted that, "Unpopular ideas can be silenced, and inconvenient facts kept dark, without the need for any official ban." This may be accomplished, he said, "because of a general tacit agreement that 'it wouldn't do' to mention that particular fact." He explained that,

> At any given moment there is an orthodoxy, a body of ideas which it is assumed that all right-thinking people will accept without question. It is not exactly forbidden to say this, that or the other, but it is 'not done' to say it, just as in mid-Victorian times it was 'not done' to mention trousers in the presence of a lady. Anyone who challenges the prevailing orthodoxy finds himself silenced with surprising effectiveness. A genuinely unfashionable opinion is almost never given a fair hearing, either in the popular press or in the highbrow periodicals.[4]

As for why this was the case, Orwell left little doubt: it had to do with media ownership. The reasons are "easy to understand," he wrote, even at that time in the 1940s. "The British press is extremely centralized, and most of it is owned by wealthy men who have every motive to be dishonest on certain important topics."

A contemporary example of the type of orthodoxy to which Orwell referred, is on the matter of Quebec sovereignty. Aside from some of the French-language media in Quebec, this concept is universally treated as an abomination. Incredibly, over the course of more than twenty years, I cannot recall a single Canadian news item, opinion column or editorial which treated self-determination for Quebeckers in a favourable or even neutral manner: all have been heavily biased against separatism.[5] Regardless of what position you take in this debate, should there not be *some* diversity of views? Of course, self-determination for "ethnic Albanians" is a different matter, as we see in Chapter Three. Now, there is unanimous support for the NATO bombing of the Federal Republic of Yugoslavia, championing a militant separatist movement known as the Kosovo Liberation Army.

In recent years, a partial list of other topics which have received orthodox coverage would include: representations of Canada as a democracy where the majority rules, free trade, feminism, national debt, immigrants, tax cuts, various 'conflicts' or wars, social program slashing, Native Canadians, globalization, welfare recipients, labour unions, competitiveness, the homeless, and protesters. In Canada, as author Linda McQuaig has documented so well, we've seen the manufacture of deficit hysteria as an excuse for slashing the social safety net.[6] Deficit hysteria was also a generalized strategy for reducing the role of government in society, increasing unemployment, driving down wages, emasculating welfare programs, undermining public health care and public education, and otherwise attacking the young, poor and downtrodden. Of course, once the annual deficits were eliminated by the neo-liberals in Ottawa, the governments of Ralph Klein in Alberta, Mike Harris in Ontario, and elsewhere, it became necessary to identify a new pretense: globalization. This became the rationale for major tax cuts, and legislation outlawing even liberal economics: the occasional deficit budgeting prescribed by John Maynard Keynes.

Instead of offering diverse perspectives on events and issues, the corporate media portray an increasingly myopic and orthodox picture of the world around us. The consistency with which they do this has its consequent, intended effect on public opinion and policy formation. American critic Michael Parenti has summed things up succinctly:

> [M]edia bias usually does not occur in random fashion; rather it moves in more or less consistent directions, favouring management over labour, corporations over corporate critics, affluent Whites over low income minorities, officialdom over protestors, the two-party monopoly over leftist third parties, privatization and free market 're- forms' over public sector development, U.S. dominance of the Third World over revolutionary or populist social change, and conservative commentators and columnists over progressive or radical ones.[7]

This is what I mean by the term *MediaThink*—it is just what the word implies—media owners, managers and workers' way of thinking, of seeing and representing events in the world around us. I coined the term a few years ago as a broader equivalent to 'group think' or the way in which people in groups tend to think alike. It is Orwell's "orthodoxy," and Antonio Gramsci's "common sense." Are these *MediaThink* perspectives absolutely universal and monolithic? Usually not. As is most apparent in the detailed analysis in Chapter Four of coverage by *The National Post*, alternative perspectives usually are available, but marginalised, and overwhelmed.

Three major questions to ask about the corporate media are: 1. *How* is it that they go about lying to us? 2. *Why* do they do so? And 3. *What* is it that they tell us and don't tell us? This is the second in a trilogy of books which began with *Common Cents*, written in 1992. Looking back nearly a decade, little has changed, only the names and places. Brian Mulroney has morphed into Jean Chretien, and Bush Senior into Bush Junior. Ken Thomson begat Conrad Black, who begat Israel Asper. Instead of Kuwait, we have Kosovo: like the alliteration, the methods and goals are still intact. *Common Cents* examined media portrayal of events such as the Gulf War, the first Ontario NDP government, and the Oka crisis. In these five case studies in this book, I attempt to show how media portrayals fall dismally short of presenting an accurate account of events, as Orwell would have it: the dishonesty of wealthy men on certain important topics. Furthermore, there is a quite discernable and consistent bias to the framework they provide, reflecting their class, gender, race, and corporate ties. *MediaThink* looks at East Timor independence, the war in Kosovo, the portrayal of women, feminism on the Supreme Court, and people of colour.

Democracy's Oxygen, which I wrote in between in 1997, focused on how and why rather than what. The questions of how and why, and what is to be done, are of course important ones, but the need for continuously documenting the orthodox bias, of continuing the work of George Orwell, Upton Sinclair, George Seldes, I.F. Stone, and Noam Chomsky, is, in my view, predominant.

I have spent more than twenty years now, studying, writing and teaching university students about the media. Initially, students are understandably resistant to the notion that "the media," (by which I mean corporate media) are lying to us. In fact, in my experience, beginning university students are far more closed to this idea than are older adults. This resistance is not surprising: it's a reflection of the myths and values propagated in the media, and in which students have been steeped, directly and indirectly, their entire lives. They too, indeed most of us are imbued with *MediaThink*.

There appears to be no end to the greed on the part of the elite. On the other hand, however effective propaganda and manipulation are, they do have limits. This is becoming apparent in the predominantly peaceful but persistent anti-globalization protests since APEC in Vancouver in 1997, continuing with Seattle in 1999, Windsor, Ontario in 2000, and Quebec City and Genoa, Italy in 2001. This movement, these young people, represent the future resistance to the orthodoxy of *MediaThink*, and the increasingly greedy, oppressive and violent powers behind it. This will be examined in my next book.

James Winter, Twin Oaks, Pelee Island Ontario, August, 2001

NOTES

1. George Orwell, "Why I Write," essay, 1947.
2. Although I indicate that these are free marketers who oppose government intervention, in fact they support massive intervention as long as it benefits corporations and the wealthy, in the form of tax credits, writeoffs, public subsidies, public support for armament industries, *et cetera*. So, contrary to representations it is not so much the presence or absence of government, as it is a matter of 'government intervention for whom?' Welfare for the poor is bad, while corporate welfare is good.
3. In fact, Russia-bashing during and just after the second world war was not a popular pastime either. Orwell wrote *1984* and *Animal Farm* because they contrasted with the pro-Soviet orthodoxy of the time. It was only later, with the promotion of the Cold War that Orwell's works were championed and became popular. As he noted in his unpublished preface to *Animal Farm*, "At this moment what is demanded by the prevailing orthodoxy is an uncritical admiration of Soviet Russia...What is disquieting is that where the USSR and its policies are concerned one cannot expect intelligent criticism or even, in many cases, plain honesty from Liberal writers and journalists who are under no direct pressure to falsify their opinions." In this of course we have come full circle, with the fall of 'communism,' in the Soviet Union, for example, the Russian war with Chechnya was unmentionable. To read Orwell's preface to *Animal Farm* entitled: "The Freedom of the Press," see

http://home.iprimus.com.au/korob/Orwell.html

4. I am indebted to Noam Chomsky for identifying this aspect of Orwell's work, in his 1989 book, *Deterring Democracy*, and elsewhere. This quotation is taken from Orwell, "The Freedom..." http://home.iprimus.com.au/korob/Orwell.html

5. For just one example, on the occasion in spring 2001 when Bernard Landry replaced Lucien Bouchard as PQ leader and Premier of Quebec, see: Kevin Dougherty, "Landry proud to be labelled 'dangerous': Klein calls the sovereigntist leader the 'most dangerous man in Canada,' to which Landry responds: 'He is damn right'," *The Ottawa Citizen*, March 5, 2001, A1.

6. Cf. any of the marvellous books by Linda McQuaig, from *Behind Closed Doors, The Quick and the Dead*, and *The Wealthy Banker's Wife*, to *Shooting the Hippo, The Cult of Impotence* and *All You Can Eat: Greed, Lust and the Triumph of the New Capitalism*.

7. Michael Parenti, "Monopoly Media Manipulation," May 16, 2001, www.michaelparenti.org/MonopolyMedia.html

CHAPTER ONE

TO WIN THEIR HEARTS AND MINDS

"I would like to convey the following, if the pro-independents do win...all will be destroyed...It will be worse than 23 years ago."
—Colonel Tono Suratman, Indonesian military commander, Dili

People had been coming to this sanctuary in Suai for months now. Close to a thousand women and children remained, milling inside Our Lady of Fatima Church and in the paved compound around it, which also contained a convent, rectory, and the shell of a cathedral which was under construction. The men had fled days earlier, after the senior parish priest Father Hilario Madeira received a warning about an impending attack, which he passed on to the refugees, telling them all to leave. Some of the women were very pregnant, and some were already nursing babies. Reportedly, they didn't feel they could flee to the hills and survive. They had nowhere else to go. Sister Mary Barudero, a nurse at the hospital in Suai, just sent four of the pregnant women back to the church two hours earlier, to await progress with their labour. "They went to the church because that's where they felt safe. They felt being near the priests was protection," Sister Barudero, 64, said later.[1]

The older children played, despite the general sense of foreboding. Shortly after 2 p.m. vehicles began arriving outside the compound, with scores of soldiers, police, and several hundred of the dreaded Laksaur [Eagle] militia. In response, many of the women and children crammed into the church, which seats 400. All of the seats were taken and people jammed the aisles. Still others remained in the compound. They closed the doors of the church and barricaded them. The militia began scaling the fence around the compound. It was 2:30 p.m.

The priests were the first to be killed. Father Tarcissus Dewanto, an Indonesian Jesuit recently ordained and posted to Suai, bravely walked out into the compound to confront the militia. First he was pushed by a milita member, and someone shouted, "Stop, he is one of ours," but then Father Tarcissus was shot from behind by another militia. He fell, dying. Father Francisco Soares came out behind him. Wielding his katana (a machete), a Laksaur militia named Americo ran over to Father Soares, and began hacking and slashing him until the red blood covered his white robes. They waited momentarily for the senior clergy, Father Hilario Madeira, to come out. When he didn't, they began looking for him. Standing on the verandah outside his room, Father Hilario, who once lived in Windsor, Ontario, saw what happened to his colleagues. He began to run across the compound towards the church, to join the women and children refugees. "And then I heard the order to shoot Father Hilario," said male nurse Eliseo Gusmao, 25. "It came from Manec Igido, a militiaman from West Timor. He saw him running. He wanted to go into the church. Manec shouted to another militiaman from Kupang, 'Muti, Muti. Shoot! Shoot! Father is there,' " Gusmao said. "I saw a militiaman strike down [Father Soares] from here," said Gusmao, pointing to his first hiding place behind an empty water tank and a banana tree in a garden not 25 metres from the scene. Manec Igido stomped on Father Hilario's lifeless body. The Catholic clergy were seen as strongly pro-independence in East Timor.

A militia leader named Lieutenant Sugito fired his pistol into the air, and gave the order to start firing. Then all hell broke loose, as the militia, police and soldiers all began firing into the crowds. As the killing went on, regular policemen, members of the police mobile brigade and army soldiers, stood outside the fence of the church compound, shooting refugees who were trying to flee.

> Inside the church, the women had barricaded the door. They were screaming and praying at once. The militia and the soldiers pushed at the door, first once, then two, three and four times. They called to the women to come out. "We want you to see your boyfriends," they said. But the women stayed inside. Then they pushed open the door and went inside with kabanas. I heard the kids inside. They were crying. A lot of children were crying inside. One woman, Aunt Maria, shouted "Rende" [I surrender], with her hands up. But the action continued without a stop. She was killed. She had a baby with her.

The attackers were armed with automatic rifles, machetes and grenades. Six or seven grenades were thrown into the church packed with refugees, according to Atanasio de Costa, a 13-year-old nephew of Father Hilario who was in the church—hiding under Father Francisco's bed—during the shooting rampage. They entered the church and sprayed the inside with automatic rifle fire. As they left, blood flowed down the doorstep.

Next, the militia set fire to the church, and Atanacio jumped through the window of Father Francisco's room and sprinted out the rear of the compound. As he was leaving, he saw two large piles of corpses behind the church. "There were dozens of bodies," Atanacio said. "They had been shot. They had been stabbed."

Eliseo Gusmao had climbed into a drainage ditch next to the convent, where he covered himself with leaves. For hours, he said, "it sounded like a war."

"I heard people screaming, people crying, people shouting," Gusmao said. Pointing at the convent, he said, "They were even pulling women away from there." At 11 p.m., after the noise subsided, Gusmao crawled out of the ditch and walked around the convent toward a row of school rooms. As he walked by one, he saw "a huge pool of blood inside." Then, as he went toward the church, he saw the carnage.

"There were more than 20 bodies piled in front of the church," he said. "Some had been shot. Some had their arms chopped off. Some had their heads chopped off. It was awful."

"I was not sure if they were dead or not, so I nudged them with my foot. But they were dead. All of them."

Gusmao quickly knelt and prayed, asking God to "receive their souls in heaven." Then he ran into the hills that surround Suai, where he remained in hiding for more than a month, subsisting on river water, bananas and cassava plants, returning only when he received word that the peacekeepers had arrived.

A pile of female underwear at the foot of the nearby cathedral's staircase afterwards appeared to indicate that dozens of women were also raped during the mayhem. Later, witnesses said the wounded and the corpses were all carted away together by the hundreds in eight large military trucks, some, such as the three priests and two dozen others, to be buried in West Timor, where they were later exhumed. Many others were dumped in crocodile-infested lakes, never to be seen again.

ORCHESTRATED CHAOS

At 10 a.m. on Saturday September 4, 1999, the United Nations announced the result of the referendum: 78.5 per cent of East Timor had voted for independence from Indonesia. Just four hours later, armed police and militias of the pro-Indonesian Laksaur group attacked the hamlet of Debos, shooting wildly and burning houses. The massacre at Our Lady of Fatima church in Suai occurred just two days later, on September 6. It is thought that at least several hundred people, almost exclusively women and children and the three priests, were murdered in the worst massacre in East Timor in that decade.

To get an idea of the extent of the carefully planned and orchestrated chaos, until the Australian-led intervention force Interfet established its control over East Timor in October that year, about 500,000 of the 850,000 population were forced to flee their homes—either to the hills of the interior where hunger and disease awaited, or across the border in a mass deportation drawn up in contingency plans by Indonesian authorities. In addition to the numerous brutal atrocities before and after the vote, an estimated 260,000 Timorans were deported to refugee camps in West Timor, in an evacuation planned by the Indonesian army.

The overwhelming vote for independence by the long-suffering people of East Timor was an extraordinary act of bravery, in the face of widespread terror and intimidation. Beginning in 1975, Indonesia first invaded then occupied and finally annexed East Timor, in defiance of official condemnation by the United Nations. Normally a referendum is not such an incredible act of bravery, but the East Timorese people were continuously harassed and brutalized by notorious pro-integration civilian militias. These groups were backed and frequently accompanied by the Indonesian armed forces, and police.

Dr. Walter Dorn is a Canadian who served with the United Nations Mission in East Timor (UNAMET) for two months, prior to the vote for independence.[2] During this time he and his colleagues personally witnessed many cases of intimidation by the militias in the southwest region of East Timor, called Suai. The militia murdered and intimidated with impunity (as well as seeming immunity) many of their political opponents, i.e., those who opposed integration with Indonesia.

Just a few weeks before the Suai massacre, Dr. Dorn stood up amidst the congregation in the Our Lady of Fatima church. He was introduced by the Reverend Francisco Soares, and Dorn told the people not to worry. He said they could vote in peace, and the United Nations would help to protect them from any reprisals.[3] "I betrayed those people who were in the church who were killed," Dr. Dorn told *The Globe and Mail* afterwards, "And the UN betrayed the East Timorese people...We were hoodwinked by the Indonesian military."

"I explained to them the measures we were taking to make sure the vote was secret," Dorn said. Following instructions from his UN superiors, he also told the people the UN would stay on in East Timor. Under an agreement from the previous May, the Indonesian army and police were to provide security for the UN mission organizing the vote. "But from the start, anti-independence militias backed by elements of the Indonesian army carried out violent attacks on civilians," *The Globe* said, afterwards.

Long afterwards, when the report of the UN Human Rights Commission was released, and still later when the entire Indonesian Human Rights Commission report was leaked, it was learned that the three militia groups called Besi Merah Putih, (BMP) Mahidi and Red Dragon always operated with an Indonesian army group.

> "Acts carried out by the Barisan Merah Putih and the military supporting them generally followed the pattern of capture, abduction, torture and murder," the [Indonesian] commission says. "While on a daily basis they threatened, robbed, terrorised and intimidated the population so that it would join the BMP and choose autonomy."[4]

According to Dr. Dorn, the militias sought to prevent certain people from voting by threatening them with death if they registered. As an example, "Jay" came to a UNAMET registration centre in the Suai region with great fear and trepidation. He said that he and his people were risking their lives by coming. As a former member of the Portuguese army and a supporter of the pro-independence forces, he had reason to be worried. His dead body was found by UNAMET staff only a few days later in his house.

Similarly, the militias told the priest in nearby Zumalai that if he continued to conduct mass in the area, he would be killed. The priest fled his parish and took refuge in the main church in Suai. Entire villages, known to be pro-independence, were uprooted at night when militias came shooting and killing. For instance, Dorn registered many of the 500 people of Laegatar in Zumalai who were displaced on July 17. They reported leaving in desperation with only what they could carry and now they feared returning home. Some of them made it to the church in Suai, where they could register at the school next door; others remained in the forest.

Intimidation was even directed against UN staff. After Dorn insisted at the outset that registration/polling sites be established in a Catholic School in Zumalai and in a village farther north in the mountains, he was accused of being a spy (for whom they did not say) and told that his security and that of his team "could not be guaranteed." Only when the UN relented two days later and accepted the site requested by militia (which was next to their base), were the threats against Dorn withdrawn. Still, most of the local staff continued to receive death threats for working with UNAMET, and many quit under such pressure.

After one of Dorn's local staff identified West Timorese who were registering with false names and birthplaces, a group of armed militia members came to his house. By that time, fortunately, he had already been tipped off and had fled (like the priest in Zumalai) to the over-crowded church grounds in Suai. The militias continued to patrol outside the church compound and threatened several times to attack it, prior to September.

Before joining UNAMET, one of the interpreters, 'Sam,' had been the subject of three attempted assassinations in Dili, the East Timorese capital where he was teaching. When Dorn visited his home village with him, many people wept at seeing him. They said that the last militia team had returned from Dili boasting that they had accomplished their job. Now the villagers saw the resurrection of Sam. "It was pleasant to see him face to face, as a UNAMET interpreter, with the man who had ordered his assassination," Dorn said. "But I still fear for his future." (Sam told Dorn he was not afraid to die working for his cause).

Before being employed by UNAMET as a driver, 'Cal' was abducted by the militias. When he refused to join he was beaten and left for dead. Later, he stopped near his home village with his UNAMET team. As with Sam, some local people were seen weeping. He explained that once someone was taken by the militias, they usually joined or turned up dead. Cal was a fortunate exception.

Many militia members come from West Timor, the Indonesian province that occupies the other half of the Island. Some of them tried to register with UNAMET using false names. Others gave correct names but claimed to be born in East Timor. One individual, after failing three times to give a correct name or birthplace, claimed eligibility by reason of marriage to an East Timorese woman in a traditional marriage. However, the woman admitted privately to UNAMET that her real husband was dead. When the militia member was refused registration, he threatened to break the windows of the registration centre, to kill local staff and to divorce his alleged wife.

Other means of general intimidation and population control included militia checkpoints at most villages. In some cases, a system of passes was set up. Some militia carried weapons, even automatic rifles, in blatant violation of the law and UNAMET guidelines. They drilled openly in playing fields and marched through the streets shouting slogans. They were most readily identified when they wore their black T-shirts with their insignia.

Many of the militia leaders were former or current policemen, soldiers or government officials. Some used their official positions to intimidate the population. The opening of mail was verified in at least one area. During registration, village chiefs (Kepala Desas) with close ties to the militia signed and stamped documents with false information stating for instance, that militia members were born in East Timor, though they openly admitted under questioning that they were born in West Timor. In some cases, the village chiefs witnessed and even made false signatures for priests and church officials in order to register a voter.

The dark plans of the militia to influence the voting on consultation day became clear during Dorn's first few days in Zumalai: they wanted to control access and intimidate people at the polling site. During the registration period, many people avoided militia and military bases, sometimes walking for hours to go around these sites. The militia would try to cordon off the area around the polling centre with rings of their members and with checkpoints on critical roads to stop people known to support independence. One man hiding in the bushes with an automatic weapon can do a lot to dissuade people from travelling along a road.

The militia leaders in also wanted to build new structures for voting. They told UNAMET these structures were to be in the traditional East

Timorese style—open on all sides. This would make it easy for militia to intimidate voters as they are about to mark their ballots. Small signals can go a long way in a society where fear is ever-present. The infamous cold stare from the local militia leader has sent a shudder down the backs of many a Timorese and even some UNAMET staff. Fortunately, the UN held firm on this one. Voting took place indoors behind specially made polling booths.

In view of what he had seen, cautioned in advance that it was vitally important that the UN conduct patrols along the roads leading to polling sites in militia-controlled areas, and introduce a United Nations peace-keeping military force to dissuade the militias "from full scale attacks." He warned that if the vote was in favour of independence, then the militia would attempt to thwart this by declaring that the ballot was unfair and even by taking up arms. Dorn said the militia in the Zumalai/Ainaro area is called Mahidi, which is an abbreviation for "Integration, Dead or Alive."

"The militias have the capability of causing widespread mayhem or even civil war," Dorn wrote in an opinion column with all this information that he submitted to *The Toronto Star* and *The Globe and Mail*, in August, 1999. Both rejected the column without comment.

AN INTERNATIONAL DISGRACE

As Elaine Briere indicates in her evocative 1996 documentary film, *Bitter Paradise*, the story of East Timor is one of the ruthless slaughter of a pastoral people, conducted with the shameless collaboration of the Canadian, American and other governments.[5] This story has been persistently ignored and/or distorted by the media for more than 25 years.

The latest installment in this campaign of murderous terror began in January, 1999. Indonesia's interim president B.J. Habibie allowed for a referendum in East Timor, with a choice between incorporation within Indonesia, (labelled as "autonomy,") or independence.

The army moved at once to prevent this [latter] outcome by terror and intimidation. In the months leading to the August referendum, 3-5000 were killed according to highly credible Church sources—twice the number of deaths prior to the NATO bombing in Kosovo, more than four times the number relative to [the] population. The terror was widespread and sadistic, intended as a warning of the fate awaiting those foolhardy enough to disregard the orders of the occupying army.[6]

Almost the entire population, 98.6%, came out to vote, despite the violence and threats, with 79% choosing independence, and with numerous documented incidents of fraudulent voting against independence. The vote led to an attempt by the militia and army to reverse the outcome by slaughter, expulsion, and razing the land. "Within two weeks more than 10,000 might have been killed."[7] After the September slaughter, the UN mission in East Timor could only account for just over 150,000 people out of an estimated population of 850,000. It reported that 260,000 "are now languishing in squalid refugee camps in West Timor under the effective control of the militias after either fleeing or being forcibly removed from their homes," and that another 100,000 were relocated to other parts of Indonesia. The rest were presumed to be hiding in the mountains.[8] In the lead-up to and aftermath of the referendum vote, Indonesia laid waste to East Timor, butchering its people.

WAS IT ALL PREVENTABLE?

Was this carnage predictable, and hence preventable? Without question. Long before the referendum, the commander of the Indonesian military in Dili, Colonel Tono Suratman, warned of what was to come: "I would like to convey the following," he said: "if the pro-independents do win...all will be destroyed...It will be worse than 23 years ago."[9] Although this particular report came out after the fact, there were also numerous indicators of the impending catastrophe, even in the corporate press.

In early May, 1999, when international agreement on the referendum was reached, an army document ordered that "Massacres should be carried out from village to village after the announcement of the ballot if the pro-independence supporters win." The independence movement "should be eliminated from its leadership down to its roots." The Australian press reported that "hundreds of modern assault rifles, grenades and mortars are being stockpiled, ready for use if the autonomy option is rejected at the ballot box." It warned that the army-run militias might be planning a violent takeover of much of the territory if, despite the terror, the populace voted for independence. Noam Chomsky comments: "All of this was understood by the 'foreign friends,' who also knew how to bring the terror to an end, but preferred evasive and ambiguous reactions that the Indonesian Generals could easily interpret as a 'green light' to carry out their work."[10]

Australian intelligence officer Andrew Plunkett later revealed that they knew precisely what was planned.

> The analysis was that the TNI [Indonesian army] would basically destroy East Timor and they'd use militia as proxies. It was quite clear the link between the militia and TNI and the militia being bit players, small pawns, and it was quite clear that they would kill a lot of people and destroy their infrastructure straight after the autonomy ballot, if [East Timor] won independence.[11]

In October, 1999, *The Sydney Bulletin* published intelligence documents demonstrating that Australian prime minister John Howard and his foreign minister Alexander Downer, were warned months beforehand that the militia was ready to "scorch" East Timor.[12] This is not surprising in light of the fact that the Australian miliary deployed about 500 "elite force" members involved in surveillance and intelligence in and around the capital of Dili and other areas of East Timor, from about April onwards.[13]

Timorese Nobel Peace Prize Laureate Jose Ramos-Horta, writing in *The International Herald Tribune* in early August, described the horrendous events which had already taken place, and predicted those which were to follow the vote.[14]

In February 1999, just a week after the Indonesian government announced it would consider allowing independence for East , *The National Post* reported that "civil war" could result if "the territory [sic] wins independence." *The Post* said "some pro-independence activists accused pro-Jakarta gangs of stockpiling guns and killing youths who refused to join [the militia]."[15]

That same month *The Toronto Star* ran a story which included an interview with militia chief Manual Sousa, near Dili, reported to be "backed by the army," and "behind a fresh reign of terror" aimed at preventing independence. "We have 10,000 members ready to go to war," Sousa said. *The Star* reported that the militia were "armed and trained by the Indonesian military."

"Sousa says his fighters are prepared to die, and kill whomever they must, to remain in Indonesia," *The Star* reported. After a local militia member was killed in fighting, Indonesian police forces brutally beat local youths in retaliation, demonstrating the support and close links between the two.[16]

In April, Timor independence leader Xanana Gusmao abandoned his position favouring a cease fire and called on his people to take up arms, when militia, "backed by the Indonesian armed forces," gunned down 17 civilians.[17] These events and dozens of others were reported by the media, sometimes because of actions by NGO groups such as Amnesty International.[18]

On August 13, *The Post* ran a story about a Canadian delegation in East Timor, sponsored by the Canadian Labour Congress and which included NDP MP Svend Robinson. The delegation reported that, "Pro-Indonesia militants, backed by the military, have unleashed a reign of terror during the campaign despite the presence of international observers." The delegation met in Jakarta with detained East Timor resistance leader Xanana Gusmao.

"He voiced concern about the violence taking place now, but particularly in the period after the vote," said Robinson, who agrees that early September could bring renewed violence. "One of the most disturbing meetings we had was with the leading pro-integration group and they quite clearly said that if they lost they expected a bloodbath."[19]

Even some high-ranking members of the military felt the disaster was preventable. Later that fall when the UN issued an apology for failing to stop the violence, retired Canadian Major-General Lewis Mackenzie, a former commander of UN forces, dismissed the apology as inadequate, saying the permanent five members of the UN Security Council—Britain, China, France, Russia and the United States—should bear responsibility for failing to stop the "mass killings." Mackenzie said the violence in East Timor was preventable. "Of all the disasters that were predictable, the one in East Timor is up around the top of the list," he said. "It was accurately predicted that independence would be favoured by the people and therefore there should have been not just contingency plans, but deployment to deal with the absolute predictable disaster—and the UN did not do that."

In reporting on this, *The National Post* noted that "Even before the outcome of the vote was announced, the chief of staff of anti-separatists forces in East Timor threatened a civil war and a slaughter of opponents if results from the referendum favoured independence."[20]

Some habitual apologists also recognized that the bloodbath was preventable. Gwynne Dyer, for example, wrote in September for the Southam newspapers that, "This post-referendum campaign of violence was entirely predictable, but the official apparatus of the UN seems to have gone into shock." Of course, Dyer went on to argue that unlike with Kosovo, the West could not intervene without the approval of the Indonesian government. Dyer wrote, "there are no volunteers for a peacekeeping force that has to shoot its way into East Timor. One way or another, you have to get Jakarta's permission first.[21] Of course, it wasn't necessary to get Slobodan Milosevic's permission—or even that of the UN—to bomb Kosovo.

Despite these clear indications to anyone combing the news media, or to any intelligence service, in important respects the western governments and media turned a blind eye to the ongoing and developing horror. Although the violence was reported on, the links between the Indonesian military and the militias generally were either assumed, ignored, or presented as unsupported allegations by pro-independence groups. The situation was more often described as one of "anarchy" or as groups fighting in a civil war, rather than the planned military operation that it was. Unlike, for example, the hue and outcry precipitated by Prime Minister Jean Chretien's shady involvement with a hotel and golf course in his home riding, or even Conrad Black's pretentious quest for a British lordship and lawsuit against the prime minister, shamelessly touted at *The Post* as a groundbreaking case in Canadian jurisprudence, (and unceremoniously tossed out by the courts) there was a distinct lack of pressure, of any clamour or campaign by the press calling for action, the absence of which amounted to tacit collusion. The right-wing media's usual political allies and collaborators such as the Reform Party were silent, as it was (apparently) not an issue of concern for them. Indeed, subsequently, Reform leader Preston Manning criticized Jean Chretien for committing 600 Canadian troops to East Timor.[22]

The international community allowed the sole responsibility for security to be left in the hands of Indonesia's military, the very source of East Timor's terror. They refused to intercede, on the grounds that they didn't wish to interfere in a matter of Indonesian internal security, or, as Gwynne Dyer indicated, that Indonesia had not given its consent. According to the Associated Press, "Even though Australia, New Zealand, France and many other countries have offered troops to a peacekeeping force, [UN Chief Kofi] Annan said all governments 'have made it clear that it's too dangerous for them to go in without the consent of Indonesia."[23]

But was this an internal matter? East Timor has never been a part of Indonesia. The Indonesian occupation of East Timor in 1975 was condemned by the Security Council of the United Nations, which demanded their immediate withdrawal. The annexation of East Timor has never been recognized by the UN, nor by the U.S. for that matter. East Timor was no more a part of Indonesia than occupied France was a part of Germany during the Second World War.

When a government-appointed Indonesian human-rights commission released a summary of its report in January, 2000, according to an article in *The Toronto Star*, "its findings stunned the international community."

> After four months of investigative work, the commission, known by its Indonesian acronym KPP-HAM, held 200 people, including then-top military chief Gen. Wiranto and five other generals, "morally responsible" for aiding a campaign of rape, murder and torture in East Timor.[24]

The findings would have stunned anyone relying on the corporate media. Knowledgeable observers and alternative media followers may have been surprised that an official Indonesian commission would actually implicate the Indonesian military. But they had long known about their culpability.

The writer for *The Toronto Star*, who was working with the UN transitional team in East Timor, quickly went on to state that "Seeking justice for East Timor is imperative, but it should not come at the cost of security in the greater region." 'Security' is a code word for maintaining a good business climate in the region. It does not refer to protecting the security of the people but rather the interests of foreign investors and global managers. Hence, for example, it means quashing nationalist movements by whatever force is necessary, under the guise of saving the nation and the region from "communism."

With the announcement of the findings of the Indonesian commission, President Abdurrahman Wahid asked for General Wiranto's resignation. (Wahid replaced the disgraced Suharto in an election in the fall of 1998. In July, 2001, Wahid himself was ousted and replaced by his deputy, Megawati Sukarnoputri, daughter of former president Achmed Sukarno, who was deposed in the 1965 coup). Initially, Wiranto demurred. While reporting on the controversy, *The Toronto Star* made scant reference to a UN report which reached similar conclusions. "A United Nations report also released yesterday blamed Indonesia's army and the militia it organized for atrocities in East Timor," was all *The Star* ever said.[25]

With Suharto deposed and his general disgraced, *The Toronto Star* and the other press could now freely refer to the history of human rights abuses by Indonesia, in East Timor. "Indonesia invaded and occupied the former Portuguese colony in 1975. Over 24 years its military was criticized for widespread human rights abuses,"[26] *The Star* said.

In 1997, despite the APEC conference protests, a trip by Foreign Affairs Minister Lloyd Axworthy to Indonesia to reassure Suharto about APEC, and the announcement that East Timorese activist Jose Ramos-Horta won the Nobel Peace Prize, almost all of *The Toronto Star's* coverage of Indonesia focussed on the Bre-X gold mining prospects and scandal, in which investors lost a bundle. The three or four stories which made reference to corruption and atrocities were the result of protests and demonstrations, or press conferences by East Timorese ex-patriats, and tended to contain denuded charges devoid of historical context or any form of verification. There was really only one story, about Jose Ramos-Horta, with any background information.[27]

During its coverage of the controversy between Wahid and Wiranto, *The Star* included a story which identified the role of the World Bank in keeping neo colonial powers in line. *The Star* commented that Wahid "is expected" to win the power struggle, because of "growing domestic and international support" for "his efforts to bring the world's fourth-most populous country its first real taste of democracy after decades of military-backed autocratic rule." The same autocratic rule, that is, which was condoned and supported by the west for all those years.

That international backing was underscored yesterday, when Wahid's government won $7 billion in aid from major donors to help pull the country out of its worst recession in 30 years. The money, however, came with a clear warning against any attempts to undermine Wahid's elected government. "It is very clear that if we came to a situation where these governance, democracy and human-rights goals were not present in the government, I don't see how there could be any financial, political or technical support from the international community," said Jean-Michel Severino, World Bank vice-president for East Asia and the Pacific, after the donor meeting.[28]

The first thing to note is that the World Bank was delighted with the Suharto government for virtually all of its decades of tenure, up until 1997-98, when even that brutal dictator balked at imposing the stringent economic conditions demanded by the IMF. Noam Chomsky described what happened, in an interview in September, 1999.

General Suharto, who had been the darling of the U.S. and the West generally ever since he took power in 1965...wiped out the main, the only popular-based political movement, a party of the left, killed hundreds of thousands of peasants, opened the place up to Western investment, virtual robbery, and that was greeted very warmly. And so it remained, through atrocity after atrocity, including the invasion of East Timor, which was supported very decisively by the U.S. and up until 1997. In 1997 he made his first mistake. One thing was he was beginning to lose control. If your friendly dictator loses control, he's not much use. The other was, he developed an unsuspected soft spot. The International Monetary Fund (IMF), meaning the U.S., was imposing quite harsh economic programs which were punishing the general population for the robbery carried out by a tiny Indonesian elite, and Suharto, for whatever reason, maybe fearing internal turmoil, was dragging his feet on implementing these. Then came a series of rather dramatic events...In February 1998, the head of the IMF, Michel Camdessus, flew into Jakarta and effectively ordered Suharto to sign onto the IMF rules...Shortly after that, in May 1998, Madeleine Albright telephoned Suharto and told him that Washington had decided that the time had come for what she called a "democratic transition," meaning, 'Step down.' Four hours later, he stepped down. This isn't just cause and effect. There are many other factors. It's not just pushing buttons. But it does symbolize the nature of the relationship.[29]

So, after was deposed, and after the vote for independence with its attendant slaughter and destruction of East Timor, and when some of the criminals are identified, then it is safe to admit in the press that the IMF and World Bank are in control. Left unsaid is the point that they were in control all along. Without the "financial, political or technical support from the international community," as the World Bank vice president indicated above, the Indonesian military and government and their militias would have withdrawn immediately from East Timor.

Even without military intelligence reports, simply by reading the press, western governments and the UN were aware of the ongoing massacres and the possibility of an approaching rein of terror. Yet, after the slaughter, the media reported that they were caught by surprise. According to *The Toronto Star*: "the Indonesian ministers seemed taken aback by what they saw. 'I don't think ministers had for one moment thought the situation was going to be this serious this quickly.' "[30]

While expressing outrage over the murders, *The Toronto Star* quickly went on to promote the "consensus view" that nothing more could have been done by the international community.

As international outrage grew, the 15 member countries on the United Nations Security Council spent more energy ruling out any "invasion" of Indonesia, than they did confronting the killers. Perhaps they were more anxious not to offend an important Asian country of 210 million people, than to save 800,000 East Timorese who had enraged the military and its armed supporters by voting for independence. Certainly, that was the message conveyed by Canada's U.N. ambassador Robert Fowler, a day after the Suai massacre. The Security Council was under pressure to do something, he agreed. But if doing something meant sending U.N. troops to Timor without Indonesia's consent, it wasn't on. "Do they mean, why can't the U.N. go to war with the fourth-largest country in the world?" he demanded. "Is that what that means? "We have all, in a variety of different ways, been trying to cajole, convince, warn the Indonesians that they must do this (assure East Timor's security), that their international reputation depends on it, and the whole world is watching." But "there is no taste in the council or in the world for going to war with Indonesia." In that, Fowler was voicing the consensus view.[31]

Of course, there could never be any reason whatsoever to go to war with Indonesia. The lessons of the Gulf War and its destruction of Iraq were not lost on Suharto, Habibie, or other U.S. client governments. A simple telephone call from Bill Clinton with a hard line approach would have ended the slaughter. As Chomsky notes,

> It would have sufficed for the U.S. and its allies to withdraw their active participation, and to inform their close associates in the Indonesian military command that the atrocities must be terminated and the territory granted the right of self-determination that has been upheld by the United Nations and the International Court of Justice.[32]

According to *The Toronto Star*, that's all it eventually took. The problem was that Clinton waited too long, failing to act until the pressure became too great to resist.

And when Clinton did finally break Indonesia's resistance to U.N. peacekeepers, all it took was a show of anger and a phone call. Nothing more. No war. He didn't put a single U.S. Marine in harm's way. Clinton's show of anger came on Sept. 9 and 10, when he described the carnage as "unacceptable," and threatened "very dire" consequences. He despatched Gen. Henry Shelton, who heads the U.S. military, to deliver an "ugly message" by telephone to his Indonesian counterpart. We don't know what Shelton said. But it got the attention of Indonesian President B.J. Habibie and his military chief, Gen. Wiranto. Jakarta folded. The next day, on Sept. 11, Habibie conceded that he had "lost control," and on Sept. 12 he invited peace-keepers to take over. The crisis was on the way to being resolved.[33]

Unfortunately, far too late for the people of East Timor. Indonesian historian John Roosa, an official observer of the vote, is quoted by Chomsky:

> "Given that the pogrom was so predictable, it was easily prevent-able...But in the weeks before the ballot, the Clinton Administration refused to discuss with Australia and other countries the formation of [an international force]. Even after the violence erupted, the Admin-istration dithered for days," until compelled by international (pri-marily Australian) and domestic pressure to make some timid gestures. Even these ambiguous messages sufficed to induce the In-donesian generals to reverse course and to accept an international presence, illustrating the latent power that has always been at hand.[34]

What is the explanation for the U.S. position? Simply and callously put, Indonesia matters and East Timor doesn't. Chomsky refers to the writing of two "Asian specialists" in *The New York Times*.

> ...the Clinton Administration, they write, "has made the calculation that the United States must put its relationship with Indonesia, a mineral-rich nation of more than 200 million people, ahead of its concern over the political fate of East Timor, a tiny impoverished ter-ritory of 800,000 people that is seeking independence."[35]

Australian foreign minister Alexander Downer "repeatedly sought to head off peacekeepers for Timor," assuring Jakarta that Indonesia was "100 times more important than East Timor."[36] As former Australian Labor PM Paul Keating said in 1995: "We are not going to hock the entire Indonesian relationship on Timor."[37]

For its part, the Canadian government indulged in the most blatant hypocrisy, when in September, 1999 Foreign Affairs Minister Lloyd

Axworthy banned future military sales to Indonesia, but exempted a military training simulator, worth the better part of $119 million dollars, to be shipped by a Canadian company to the Indonesian air force at the height of the post-referendum violence. This sale was worth more than all cumulative known Canadian military sales to Indonesia. A memo released to the East Timor Alert Network (ETAN) under the Freedom of Information Act one year later indicated Ottawa was reluctant to cancel an export permit for the shipment because officials feared the company would sue the federal government in retaliation. Hence, Axworthy's ban did not cover sales for which permits had already been issued.[38]

When western governments finally acted, it was the result of public horror and popular political pressure. The Australian government is given credit for pushing U.S. President Bill Clinton, but it took the Australian people to move their government. Here's Australian film maker John Pilger, writing in *The Guardian*:

> When the Australian government was finally persuaded to provide troops to a UN peacekeeping force, it was only after East Timor had been devastated and de-populated by Indonesian-run death squads and only after public opinion in Australia forced the issue. Tens of thousands demonstrated, trade unions boycotted Indonesian cargo, schools stopped. It was one of those wonderful moments when the force of popular moral and political outrage cannot be ignored or distracted; it was Australians at their best.[39]

Yet, this devastation of East Timor has entered the media and political annals as a model of success for international peacekeeping. As *The National Post* indicated, "The [International Institute of Security Studies] insists peacekeeping can work when regional powers take a real interest. For example, Australian involvement in East Timor in 1999 quickly halted the wave of killings by Indonesian-backed militias."[40]

This perspective was reinforced when Federal Minister of Defense Art Eggleton announced a new "quick in and out" peacekeeping strategy in

2001. Eggleton used East Timor as an example, reinforcing the by-now-standard view that western governments acted quickly and effectively. "As examples of the new approach, Mr. Eggleton cited the current six-month mission...to the Horn of Africa...along with September 1999's six-month deployment to East Timor," *The National Post* reported.[41] But while there eventually may have been some successes with peacekeeping in East Timor, one of them was not the timing. The delay, the lack of concern, was an intentional horror which eclipses any aspect which was 'successful.' Additionally, as Walter Dorn notes of the Australian-led Interfet force, neighbours do not make good peacekeepers: it should be someone without a vested interest.[42]

THE EVENTS OF 1965

Here is a brief recounting of some of the history, the events which happened prior to 1999, which were either left out altogether by the media or given scant reference in a sentence or two.

By September 1965, the Indonesian Communist Party (PKI) had become the largest Communist party outside the Soviet Union and China. It numbered more than 3.5 million, with an affiliated membership of some 10 million. Trade unions, women's groups, artists and peasant organisations were also growing at a spectacular rate.[43]

That month the Indonesian military, which was being advised, equipped, trained, and financed by the U.S. military and the CIA, overthrew President Achmed Sukarno (father to current president Megawati Sukarnoputri) in a coup, with the slaughter of somewhere between one half million and a million members of the mass-based Indonesian Communist Party, along with suspected leftists, and ordinary peasants.[44] The coup deposed Sukarno and installed General Suharto in his place. The generals also destroyed hundreds of clinics, libraries, schools, and community centres established by the Communists. According to a CIA study, "in terms of numbers killed," the 1965-66 massacres in Indonesia "rank as one of the worst mass murders of the 20th century."[45]

Bertrand Russell wrote after the events: "In four months, five times as many people died in Indonesia as in Vietnam in 12 years."[46] Noam Chomsky described the results and the response:

> Army-led massacres slaughtered hundreds of thousands in a few months, mostly landless peasants, destroying the mass-based political party of the left, the PKI. The achievement elicited unrestrained euphoria in the West and fulsome praise for the Indonesian "moderates," Suharto and his military accomplices, who had cleansed the society and opened it to foreign plunder.[47]

In an article in *The New York Times* in March 1966, Max Frankel described U.S. President Lyndon Johnson's delight with the situation and noted that Washington's expectations were finally being realized.[48]

This was fairly important background information in the summer of 1999, at a time when East Timor was voting on independence from Indonesia, and militia groups, backed by the Indonesian military, were slaughtering civilians to deter them from voting for independence. Yet, even the relatively "progressive" *Toronto Star* newspaper made just two brief references to Sukarno in all of 1999, both identifying his daughter, who was running for election. "Megawati Sukarnoputri, the popular daughter of Indonesia's first president Sukarno" was all *The Star* said.

Indeed, in all of its coverage in 2000 as well, *The Star* only had one reference to Sukarno and the 1965 coup, in an opinion piece by neoliberal journalism professor David Van Praagh, who wrote:

> But since it declared and won independence from returning Dutch colonialists in 1945-49, and barely escaped a successful Communist coup in 1965, Indonesia has not been at peace with itself. Years of stifling conformity under the army and the pretentious icon Suharto followed years of dangerous turmoil under the leftist demagogue Sukarno.[49]

Van Praagh overlooks the role of the CIA, the military coup and all of the deaths, in his single-minded focus on a narrowly-averted "communist coup." The murderous dictatorship of Suharto is reduced to nothing more than "stifling conformity" and "pretentiousness," in comparison with the "dangerous turmoil" under the "leftist demagogue Sukarno," who was in fact a moderate nationalist.[50]

Van Praagh is in good company. The 1965 Indonesian slaughter has been virtually ignored by the Canadian and American media since it happened.

THE 1975 OCCUPATION

In the mid 1970's, Portugal dismantled its colonial empire, including East Timor, and Indonesia immediately moved in. In 1975 Indonesia had a population of 136 million versus East Timor's 700,000 people. Indonesia first tried to block Timorese independence by backing a coup in the territory, but when this failed it launched a full-scale invasion of East Timor in December 1975, using the pretext that it was maintaining order in a civil war.[51] In fact the very brief civil war had ended by August 1975 with a Fretilin (Timor nationalist) victory, and was over long before the invaders landed.[52]

The U.S. gave Suharto the green light for his invasion, armed the Indonesian forces, and at the United Nations, U.S. ambassador Daniel Patrick Moynihan successfully worked, as he later boasted in his memoirs, to make sure the international organization was ineffective in challenging Jakarta's aggression. Despite these efforts, the UN has never recognized Indonesia's annexation of East Timor.

Since that time, Suharto and Indonesia conducted the mass genocide of one third or more of the population of East Timor, variously estimated at between 200,000 to 300,000 people.

'FAILING TO WIN THEIR HEARTS AND MINDS'

Elsewhere, American authors have demonstrated the glaring biases and "language of apologetics" of American media such as *The New York Times*.[53] It's instructive to take a very brief look at the way in which these historical events have been covered in the Canadian media. John Stackhouse is a reporter for *The Globe and Mail* who is widely viewed as a progressive, if not bleeding-heart liberal. He was *The Globe and Mail* development issues reporter through the 1990s, and the author in 2000 of the [bizarrely titled] book *Out of Poverty and Into Something More Comfortable*. The publisher's blurb on his book notes that "From East Timor to Timbuktu, John Stackhouse has met and lived with hundreds of the world's poor." *The Toronto Star* book reviewer described him as "a liberal-minded if somewhat jaundiced journalist."[54] A book reviewer for the *Waterloo* (Ontario) *Record* gushed: "I'm not the only one who thinks [Stackhouse] is the best reporter in Canada, a national treasure."

In January 1996, Stackhouse tacked on a five day visit to East Timor following Prime Minister Jean Chretien's 'Team Canada' trade mission to Jakarta Indonesia. Writing in *The Globe*, Stackhouse noted the ferocity of the 1975 invasion of East Timor, but labelled it a "crackdown" and lamented the world's indifference, oblivious to the fact that this included his own, 'world class' newspaper.

> It has been 20 years since Indonesian troops marched into Dili and launched one of the century's most ferocious crackdowns on a civilian population...With indifference from the rest of the world, Indonesia has been able to crush much of the resistance in the former Portuguese colony, which it invaded in 1975 and annexed as its 27th province in 1976.[55]

In the 28th paragraph of his article, Stackhouse finally mentions and then immediately excuses the genocide.

> There also is the issue of the estimated 200,000 people who died following the Indonesian invasion, although most of those deaths were linked to famine and the mass movement of people through inhospitable, malaria-ridden hills.

Ah, if only those foolish East Timorese people had the good sense to *stay out of* those malaria-ridden hills! It probably had little to do with the murderous

25

Indonesian forces and the local militia forces of the time who were chasing them.

In the next paragraph, Stackhouse launches into the language of full blown apologetics, describing Indonesia as a valued ally and linchpin of moderation.

To the West, however, Indonesia is a valued ally and trading partner, a linchpin of moderation in the Islamic world, a rock of stability in Southeast Asia, a key source of important emerging markets. What's more, the nation has won a trophy room full of awards for its success in primary education and health care.

Remember, this is after 30 years of brutal, murderous dictatorship, which in just two years' time would be brought to an end with Suharto—whom Stackhouse was toasting—deposed, disgraced, and charged with massive fraud and theft.

In the first article in his series, run on the front page, Stackhouse did describe Suharto's informal transmigration policy, shipping thousands of young Timorese to far-flung islands, "to dilute the Timorese identity," all the while "outsiders have taken control of the economy." He failed to mention that the reason for this action was to undermine Timorese continuing resistance to Indonesia's brutal occupation. Although he mentioned the Indonesian invasion in 1975, there was no mention at all of the hundreds of thousands of deaths since then. Instead, he wrote:

Since [1975], the [Indonesian] government *has failed to win the hearts and minds* of most East Timorese, especially the disgruntled youth who see few economic prospects.[56]

So, for this liberal and sympathetic Canadian journalist, this national treasure and his editors, the mass genocide by Suharto is euphemistically summed up as failing "to win the hearts and minds" of the Timorese people.

Finally, for our purposes here, Stackhouse took a swipe at those such as Noam Chomsky who "rant" that the media have distorted the story of

Indonesia and East Timor, oblivious to the fact that his own series proves Chomsky's point.

> On North American university campuses, the invasion of East Timor has played well. There's a David and a Goliath. And there's Noam Chomsky: The American intellectual's rant about how the corporate-controlled media allegedly ignore East Timor has ignited an intellectual spark enjoyed by few ethnic struggles.

It's as if, thanks to Chomsky, the "ethnic struggle" in East Timor has garnered more attention than it deserves!

Two years to the day after the referendum vote and accompanying massacres, 93% of the people of East Timor voted for a constituent assembly. Up to 425,000 people elected an 88-member assembly, which will draft a constitution and become the first parliament by December, 2001. The Associated Press said on August 30, "there is little doubt that the Revolutionary Front for an Independent East Timor, [FRETILIN] which led the country's independence struggle, would win a comfortable majority and obtain a clear mandate to form the new government." Presidential elections are expected in March or April, 2002.

NOTES

1. I relied on a variety of sources to pull together this account of what happened in the Suai massacre. Cf. Tom Fawthrop, "Man behind Timor massacre named," *The Age*, [Melbourne], November 5, 1999; http://www.etan.org/et99c/november/01-6/5man.htm; Doug Struck, "Nun tells of massacre by militia at church," *The Washington Post*, September 11, 1999; Ningrum Widyastuty, "Blood of victims seeped out of church," *The Sydney Morning Herald*, September 13, 1999; Hamish McDonald, "Masters of Terror: Crimes Against Humanity in East Timor," *The Sydney Morning Herald*, April 28, 2001.
   http://www.smh.com.au/news/0104/28/text/review1.html; Max Stahl, "'They killed mainly women and children and old men': Investigators this week discovered 26 bodies—evidence of the Sept. 6 massacre of three priests and hundreds of refugees they were trying to protect in Suai's simple Catholic church," *The National Post*, November 27, 1999.

2. This account is taken, sometimes verbatim, with permission from Walter Dorn, "The Dangerous Militias in East Timor," Peace Studies Program, Cornell University 26

August 1999. Dr. Dorn is a Senior Fellow at Cornell University and a faculty member of the Pearson Peacekeeping Centre in Clementsport Nova Scotia. He has also served as the UN representative of Science for Peace since 1983. This article was rejected without comment by *The Toronto Star* and *The Globe and Mail*, less than a week before the independence vote in East Timor. I am grateful for Dr. Dorn's comments on, and assistance with, this chapter. Any mistakes which remain are my responsibility alone.

3. Quoted in Paul Knox, "Terror in East Timor: 'UN betrayed Timorese,' Canadian charges: Election official regrets his role," *The Globe and Mail*, September 13, 1999. Also verified by personal correspondence.

4. Quoted in Hamish McDonald, "Masters of Terror..."

5. Bitter Paradise: The Sellout of East Timor, produced and narrated by Elaine Briere, Video, Canada, 56 minutes.
   http://www.workingtv.com/real/realBitterParadise.html. For an historical overview and evidence of gendercide, see also, http://www.gendercide.org/case_timor.html

6. Noam Chomsky, "East Timor Retrospective," Z-Net, www.zmag.org, September 27, 1999.

7. Chomsky, "East Timor Retrospective."

8. Noam Chomsky, "East Timor Is Not Yesterday's Story," Z-Net, www.zmag.org, Oct 23, 1999.

9. Chomsky, "East Timor Retrospective."

10. *Ibid.* Chomsky does not footnote his sources in this publication.

11. John Land, "East Timor: A nation betrayed," *Green Left Weekly*, May 23, 2001. See also Lansell Taudevin and Jefferson Lee (Ed) *East Timor: Making amends? Analysing Australia's role in reconstructing East Timor*, Otford Press, Sydney, 2001.

12. John Pilger, "A moral outrage: It was the public, not politicians, who forced the Australian government to end the betrayal of East Timor, *The Guardian*, Nov. 2, 1999.

13. Ian Hunter, "Australia's elite forces scouted Timor since April," The *Sydney Morning Herald*, October 10, 1999.
    http://pandora.nla.gov.au/parchive/1999/S1999-Oct-21/www.easttimor.com/DOCS/archives/0720.htm

14. Jose Ramos-Horta, "Indonesian Militia Promote Widespread Intimidation, Violence and Terror in East Timor, to Influence August 30th Vote," www.flipside.org, August 16, 1999. See also, "Indonesian Army Rigging East Timor Vote," *Flipside*, June 25, 1999; John Land, "Militia violence Continues in East Timor," *Green Left Weekly*, July 7, 1999.

15. Lewa Pardomuan, "East Timor becomes a tinderbox: Independence fever has residents bracing for civil war," *The National Post*, February 2, 1999.

16. Martin Regg Cohn, "East Timor teeters on brink of civil war Civilian militia fights to prevent Indonesia from severing ties," *The Toronto Star*, February 20, 1999.

17. Terry Friel, "East Timor leader calls for end to ceasefire: 'No other alternative'" *The National Post*, April 6, 1999.

18. See, "Threat to 'cleanse' supporters of independence: East Timor in panic: Disarm militias before it's too late, Amnesty warns," *The National Post*, April 30, 1999.

19. Mike Trickey, "Canada ignoring East Timor terror, delegation says," The Victoria *Times Colonist*, August 13, 1999.

20. Francine Dube, "UN issues apology for deadly bungling: Third plea for forgiveness in six weeks: Mackenzie calls move inadequate, says Security Council must take responsibility," *The National Post*, December 31, 1999.

21. Gwynne Dyer, "West can't go into East Timor the way NATO did in Kosovo," Victoria *Times Colonist*, September 11, 1999.

22. Sandra Cordon, "Canadians won't be in Timor for month," The Victoria *Times Colonist*, September 17, 1999.

23. Patrick McDowell, AP, "UN under siege in East Timor: Troops, militiamen menace compound; Annan calls for foreign intervention," *The Herald-Leader*, September 11, 1999.

24. Susan Lynne Tillou, "The Path To Justice In East Timor," *The Toronto Star*, March 16, 2000.

25. "Indonesia: General to be Sacked," *The Toronto Star*, February 1, 2000.

26. Geoff Spencer, "Minister refuses call to resign: Indonesian rejects blame in East Timor atrocities," *The Toronto Star*, February 2, 2000.

27. Cf. Paul Watson, "Fighting for the freedom to choose," *The Toronto Star*, January 19, 1997; Allan Thompson, "East Timor survivors tell Ottawa of atrocities: Torture, murder cited as reason to keep Suharto out," *The Toronto Star*, November 13, 1997; Allan Thompson, "Activists appeal for Axworthy support: East Timorese urge halt to military exports to Indonesia," *The Toronto Star*, July 30, 1997.

28. Jonathan Thatcher, "Wiranto defies order to resign: Indonesian general attends Indonesian cabinet meeting," *The Toronto Star*, February 3, 2000.

29. Noam Chomsky, "East Timor on the Brink," Interviewed by David Barsamian, KGNU Radio, Boulder Colorado, September 8, 1999. <www.zmag.org>

30. Allan Thompson, "Diplomat raises fears of genocide in Timor: Canadian saw few men among 25,000 refugees in camps," *The Toronto Star*, September 16, 1999.

31. "The phone rang too late for Timor," *The Toronto Star*, September 17, 1999.

32. Chomsky, "East Timor Retrospective."

33. "The phone rang too late for Timor," *The Toronto Star*, September 17, 1999.

34. Chomsky, "East Timor Retrospective."

35. *Ibid.*

36. John Pilger, "A moral outrage."

37. Sean Healy, "Were the Media Really on East Timor's Side?" *Green Left Weekly*, October 6, 1999. www.greenleft.org.au/. See also www.asiet.org.au/

38. Paul Knox, "Ottawa slow to block arms to Indonesia: Ministry memo suggests government feared lawsuit from Canadian firm preparing to ship military gear during conflict in East Timor," *The Globe and Mail*, August 30, 2000. See also the ETAN web site http://www.etan.ca/etannews/etannews_52_2000aug31.shtml#3

39. John Pilger, "A moral outrage."

40. Corinna Schuler, "West accused of shunning African peacekeeping: Military think-tank report," *The National Post*, May 17, 2001.

41. Mike Blanchfield, "Eggleton set to trim peace missions 'Early in/early out': Canada would do short stints, leave long haul to others," *The National Post*, March 22, 2001.

42. Walter Dorn, personal communication, August, 2001.

43. James Balowski, "East Timor: revisiting Indonesia's brutal past," *Green Left Weekly*, September 22, 1999.

44. Michael Parenti, "Monopoly Media Manipulation," May, 2000. http://www.michaelparenti.org/MonopolyMedia.html

45. Stephen R. Shalom, Noam Chomsky, and Michael Albert, "East Timor Questions & Answers," *Z Magazine*, October, 1999.

46. Quoted in James Balowski, "East Timor: revisiting Indonesia's brutal past," *Green Left Weekly*, September 22, 1999.

47. Noam Chomsky, "East Timor Retrospective," Z-Net, www.zmag.org, September 27, 1999.

48. Quoted in James Balowski, "East Timor."

49. David Van Praagh, "Hope for democracy is alive in Indonesia," *The Toronto Star*, February 13, 2000.

50. Shalom et al., "East Timor…"

51. Shalom et al., "East Timor…"

52. Edward Herman and David Peterson, "How *The New York Times* Protects Indonesian Terror in East Timor," *Z Magazine*, July, 1999.

53. Herman and Peterson, "How *The New York Times*…"

54. *The Toronto Star* reviewer did note: "For readers who want context for these vignettes, this book will frustrate. It beats me, for instance, how any journalist, even from the business press, would barely notice the colonial backdrop that doomed many of Stackhouse's destinations." Marlene Webber, "Back from the wars," *The Toronto Star May 14, 2000*.

55. John Stackhouse, "Destino," *The Globe and Mail*, February 3, 1996.

56. John Stackhouse, "Timorese become strangers at home," *The Globe and Mail*, February 2, 1996. (Emphasis added.)

CHAPTER TWO

FEMINISM DID IT

"It's not that she was a bad person, she just led a crazy life. She met up with the wrong kind of people."
—Bill Pretanski, stepfather of Tracey Lynn Kelsh

Tracey Lynn Kelsh lived just down the street in Windsor from my partner, Gail Robertson, in the early '90s. Tracey, 22, was a high school friend of Elizabeth Graham, my former teaching assistant. In October, 1994, Tracey was murdered in her apartment by her boyfriend of about one month, Dennis James Edgar, 30. Following a violent struggle in which the sink was torn from the wall and water sprayed everywhere, Edgar held police at bay outside the bathroom, while he apparently slashed Tracey's throat with a knife. By the time the police got into the bathroom, it was too late for Tracey, who died of multiple stab wounds.

Edgar's father, Dennis Sr., was murdered late in 1993. In September, 1994, just a month before the murder of Tracey Lynn Kelsh, three Windsor women were found guilty of the second degree murder of Dennis Edgar Sr., by an Ontario Court jury.

Staff reporter Chuck Sinkevitch of *The Windsor Star* was assigned to cover the story of Tracey Lynn Kelsh's murder. Sinkevitch went to the scene of the murder and interviewed bystanders who lived in the same building.

31

Later, he interviewed Staff Sergeant Lloyd Grahame, of the Windsor Police, and he drove to Forest Glade on the east side of Windsor, to interview Tracey's step-father. Here's the way Sinkevitch's story began two days later on the front page of *The Star*. A black and white photograph showed Tracey's body being carried out on a stretcher.

HER PATH BECAME 'A DEATH SPIRAL'
TRAGIC ENDING TO A 'CRAZY LIFE.'

As a kid, Tracey Lynn Kelsh had a hard time obeying the crossing guards when she walked to school. From there, she followed her own path, a path into what her stepfather Bill Prestanski called 'a death spiral.' "Tracey is a textbook case of someone in society that didn't want to go along with the standard way of doing things," he said from his home in Forest Glade, late Monday night. "She always said she could take care of herself. I guess she was wrong." Early Sunday morning, 22-year-old Tracey Lynn Kelsh became the city's second murder victim of the year. Police said her throat was slashed during a violent struggle. It was the end of the line for a local girl who grew up too fast, her stepfather said, and turned her back on those who wanted to help her get her life back on track.[1]

Obviously, anyone who has a hard time obeying crossing guards is just asking for it.

The story was almost exclusively about Tracey, and how she turned her own life into a "death spiral," and brought on her own death. The information source for all of this was almost exclusively her stepfather Bill Prestanski. "Prestanski, who married Tracey's mother Patti more than 10 years ago, said the family had no choice but to watch when Tracey ran away at 14, and when she had the first of three children two years later."

"With only a Grade 8 education, Ms. Kelsh eventually turned to exotic dancing as a way to pay the rent and feed three children. It became a routine, but she kept in touch with her family, Prestanski said, up until about a month ago." *The Star's* story then made its first mention of the perpetrator.

"It was then, he said, that Tracey got a new boyfriend."

There were just three more brief references to Dennis Edgar in the story, sprinkled amongst the details of Tracey's exotic table top dancing. (Paragraph numbers are in parentheses).

"Dennis James Edgar, 30, was arraigned Sunday night on a charge of second-degree murder and will appear in court again this week." (11)

"They were locked in the bathroom and he was holding the door closed. Our officers couldn't get in." (21)

"The accused's father, Dennis Sr., was murdered last year. Late last month, three Windsor women were found guilty of second degree murder by an Ontario Court jury." (26)

Meanwhile, we learned that Tracey left home at 14, and didn't have custody of her three children, but visited them regularly. She worked as a freelance "exotic" (table top) dancer at strip clubs in Windsor, including *Studio 4*, and *Silver's*, where she was known as "Kayla."

"She was good at going where the money was the best," said an anonymous manager at one of the clubs.

"It's not that she was a bad person, she just led a crazy life. She met up with the wrong kind of people," her stepfather said.

Tracey Lynn Kelsh was the victim in a brutal murder. This front page story in *The Windsor Star* blamed Tracey for her own death. This is what is known as blaming the victim, or "victimization." Was there another perspective on Tracey's life and death? Had she no friends or relatives who could have told a different story, for example, about why she ran away from her stepfather's home at 14? I wonder if the story might have been pursued from the obvious angle of her boyfriend's life: the murder of his father, evidently by three women, how this affected him psychologically, how his life became a death spiral for an innocent victim. Why would none of this occur to the reporter and his editors?

At this writing in July 2001, Dennis James Edgar still has not been brought to trial. The venue has been changed to London, Ontario, because of the alleged prejudicial effect of the news reporting of the case, on his trial.

WAY COOL

I remember that morning quite vividly: awakening, fetching the paper from my front walk, and sitting down to read it over a cup of coffee. As I slipped the paper from its plastic wrapper and unfolded the front section, a front page story caught my eye. Leapt out at me, actually. The headline read: "Cools blames moms for male violence: Women's Day meeting ends in anger."

It was March 8, 1995, less than six months after Tracey Lynn Kelsh's murder. It was International Women's Day, and the paper was the Toronto *Globe and Mail*. The CP story reported on comments made by Senator Anne Cools, at a meeting in Ottawa the previous day. Cools reportedly said she has learned that the relationship between a mother and a son who grows up to become violent is "one side of the equation that's grossly overlooked. And I want to leave with all of you here, that behind every abusing husband is an abusing mother."

I had two reactions to this story. On the one hand, I was incredulous. Why would senator Cools make these comments? Where was she getting her information from? The story didn't help much in this regard, telling us that "Ms. Cools cited no specific studies to support her position, which was contradicted by critics, including Lesley Ackrill, who works in a Toronto shelter for abused women and children." The story *did* quote these critics. But it also gave considerable ink and prominence to Cool's charges. *The Globe* quoted Ms. Ackrill as saying, "Studies show it's more likely that boys grow up to be abusers if they see their fathers abusing their mothers. What we see from the boys who come to this shelter is that they pattern themselves after their fathers."[2] *Statistics Canada* agrees with Ms. Ackrill rather than Senator Cools. The federal agency reported in 1996 that fathers are responsible for 73 per cent of physical assaults and 98 per cent of sexual assaults on children, despite the far greater exposure to children by mothers.[3]

It was deja vu all over again. In 1993, *New York* magazine chose March 8, International Women's Day, to run their special report, "Crying Rape: The Politics of Date Rape on Campus."

"There are growing questions about how real the campus rape threat is and how much of the controversy is fuelled not so much by psychosexual concerns as by political ones," wrote Peter Hellman.[4]

Anne Cools is a media darling. The first Black woman senator, she was appointed in 1984 by Pierre Trudeau, after she ran unsuccessfully as a Liberal candidate in two federal elections in Toronto. Although Senator Cools was once jailed over a university protest in the 1960's, has worked in women's shelters, and was a social worker, she has "the right stuff." Cools has quoted, approvingly, from U.S. conservative Supreme Court Justice Clarence Thomas, in the Senate, to the effect that some Black people, in their "intellectual and political outlook do not necessarily conform to stereotypes." That is, they adopt right-wing positions which disadvantage and do not represent the vast majority of people of colour, and women.[5] Of course, those who do this, from Thomas to Cools, to right-wing Black columnist Thomas Sowell, are celebrated by the media.

On the other hand, I was angry that *The Globe and Mail* would run these ridiculous statements on their front page, on International Women's Day. As I recall, it was the only International Women's Day story, if you can call it that. What kind of news judgement was this? It was insulting and demeaning to women to promote these unsubstantiated charges by a men's rights advocate at any time, but especially on that day.

The very next day, *The Globe* did backtrack somewhat, indicating in a less prominent follow up story that "among the reams of competing research statistics, there is little to back [Cool's] contentious claim that men who beat their wives were as children the victims of battering mothers." The story quoted Senator Cools as saying, "My evidence is 20 to 25 years working in the field, working with people in these circumstances. That is my evidence." *The Globe* stated that "Academics have squabbled over the definition of abuse," and cited a *Statistics Canada* study, and then an academic criticizing it. As if this were a mere "squabble." It then went on to say that, "If she has detractors, the controversial senator can also claim allies," and quoted a sociologist.

> Reena Sommer, a sociologist at the University of Manitoba who dismisses the Statscan study of family violence as "biased" and "seriously flawed," has conducted research that shows men and women perpetrate violence against each other at an equal rate. While men injure women more seriously, she maintains, women compensate for their disadvantage in size and strength by using weapons against men.[6]

So, *The Globe's* narrative on all this was that the evidence is mixed. A few weeks later, Senator Cools was back in the news when she dug up some studies to support her allegations, and blamed, as the headline indicated, "feminist ideologues for obscuring women's role in domestic violence." *The Globe* presented Cool's account of the research, interviewed one or two academics who qualified the results somewhat, but who were also in agreement, including one male researcher who "welcomed Ms. Cools' efforts to rekindle debate over child abuse and condemned society's 'total neglect of the female capacity to be aggressive, as a great loss to the debate and to women.'" *The Globe* then concluded: "there appears to be a growing number of academics who, like Ms. Cools, feel the feminist agenda has produced research that is biased against men on the subject of domestic violence."[7]

In 1997, Senator Cools was in the news again, this time getting a sympathetic hearing for her views that it's mothers who murder babies.

> A baby's killer is often the most unlikely suspect—its mother, says a child-welfare advocate. Studies and the history of child abuse show that the perpetrators of infanticide and neglected children are most often mothers, Senator Anne Cools said yesterday.[8]

The Globe and Mail's resident antifeminist, Margaret Wente, was so taken with Cools that she devoted a column to lionizing her. Wente said you have to be "either fearless or idiotic" to wade into the area of family abuse, but somehow implied Cools was the former. "Meet Senator Anne Cools—former feminist hero, current feminist goat, and new champion of men's rights," Wente wrote.[9] Well, what stance would *The Globe's* only woman news columnist take? Would she side with the feminists or men's rights groups? Proving the adage that only men-in-skirts get promoted to management positions in the media, Wente made her position quite clear. In a remarkable display of historical revisionism, Wente wrote that when Cools first made her allegations, "Women's groups had conniptions," which is true enough, but also that "Reporters quickly summoned experts who said Ms. Cools was not only dead wrong, but had perhaps lost her marbles." In this way, although she was distorting her own newspaper's coverage, Wente supported the conservative myth that the press is liberal and unduly influenced by 'special interest groups' such as the women's movement. (Well, as that American bumper sticker reads: "The press is only as liberal as the conservative corporations that own them.") Wente next went on to espouse (through Cools) another conservative myth: feminists have gone radical.

> How did Anne Cools change from champion of battered women to renegade antifeminist? Ms. Cools argues she hasn't changed at all. It's the women's movement that has. "The radicals have hijacked the agenda," she said two years ago. "They see men as evil, and will stop at nothing to ensure the superiority of women."

Wente next staked out her position backing Cools. "Ms. Cools is definitely capable of overstatement. But on several important points, she's right." In defiance of *Statistics Canada*, police reports and the vast bulk of academic work, Wente continued, "Do mothers abuse their sons? Of course they do. The most reputable studies of family violence have found that mothers physically and verbally abuse their children more often than fathers do."

Then why all of the controversy? Because, Wente said, "it is greatly threatening to people who have a large investment in a world view of men as perpetrators and women as victims. Many feminists, however, will never forgive her for saying so."

Thus, Wente clearly championed the cause of men's rights, in what for her was a typical approach. I do not have the space here to elaborate on Wente's antifeminist role at *The Globe,* using any of a plethora of available examples. Suffice to say that I have labelled her as "antifeminist" on the basis of dozens of examples, as a perusal of her columns demonstrates.[10]

THE WAR ON FEMINISTS

There are numerous ways in which the media undermine feminists and women generally. As with visible minorities, one way is by largely excluding women (let alone feminists) from parity in newsrooms, let alone management and leadership roles in news organizations.[11] In addition, the media such as *The Globe and Mail* use three central methods in their war on feminists. The first means, which Anne Cools exemplifies, is to find quotable public persona, and use them to cudgel the opposition, in this case feminists. This is an old journalistic trick, amply demonstrated when Senator Joseph McCarthy was used to thrash the alleged "communists" in the U.S. in the 1950s. When someone in authority says something the media are anxious to hear, it is quotable and reportable by virtue of this very fact, regardless of whether there is any evidence to support them. On the other hand of course, all the statistics in the world won't get you a hearing in the media if your arguments don't 'have resonance.' Authoritative sources are not limited to senators, but may include other politicians, neo-liberal academics, business leaders, authors, and anyone with "the right stuff."

To be fair to the media, as we will see, there is a very well-heeled lobby group which is promoting the antifeminist cause. Part of the reason for its success is *MediaThink*, but it also has to do with funding and massive public relations campaigns which the media would find difficult to resist, even if they wanted to.

The second method is to hire people like Margaret Wente, who will espouse her perspective *ad nauseam*, and which is indistinguishable from that of conservative White males, periodically sprinkling her columns with the views of those very same men, or other men-in-skirts such as Senator Cools.[12]

The third method, and one I will address later in the chapter, has been perfected by minions at *The National Post*, and that is to take reputable academic research and distort it out of all recognition and proportion, to the chagrin of its authors, in order to further your own antifeminist and misogynist agenda.

FOR THE SAKE OF THE CHILDREN

Returning to Anne Cools, early in 1997 she single handedly kept Bill C-41 gridlocked in the Senate for more than two weeks. The bill contained Allan Rock's changes to the Divorce Act, changes which Cools saw as prejudicial to men. Cools was able to do this because the Liberals only had a one-seat majority in the Senate at the time. She and her Conservative cohorts succeeded in softening the bill's measures, and got the government to agree to a Joint Committee on Custody and Access, which eventually crossed the country for two years, holding hearings. Those hearings became a circus sideshow, with Cools and committee co-chair Roger Gallaway ridiculing the women who testified. Liberal MP Gallaway reportedly, "openly boasted to reporters of his bias toward fathers' rights activists."[13] Periodically during the hearings, the media would pick up on the story of one or other poor father who didn't have access to his children, while ignoring the plight of women who came before the committee. As Michele Landsberg wrote in *The Toronto Star*, "The committee, brain-child of controversial Liberal Senator Anne Cools, appears, in the wake of the hearings, to have been a platform for embittered fathers' rights activists."[14]

Like the Robin Williams role in the 1993 Fox film *Mrs. Doubtfire*, the story line of the committee and the media was that men are loving creatures who just want to be with their kids, while women (Sally Fields) are anal-retentive creatures who can't stand a messy house.[15] Of course, some men are loving and some women are anal-retentive, and vice-versa. But when will Robin don a wig and play a single mom whose ex-husband refuses to see the kids and refuses to pay support? Single moms in films are far more likely to be Julia Roberts as Erin Brockovich: beautiful, thin, busty women who break men's balls to further their careers, meanwhile abandoning their children to loving, dishwashing male boyfriends. How typical!

The Cools Committee report, with the Orwellian title, *For the Sake of the Children*, recommended an end to the tradition of giving preference to mothers when awarding custody of children after a divorce, and to the "tender years doctrine," which holds that very young children are best left in the care of their mothers. It reportedly endorsed the legal concept of "shared parenting," which would give mothers and fathers equal parenting rights after divorce. After much controversy, the Liberal government announced in May 1999 that it would delay making changes to child custody laws until May of 2002, or later. According to the press this 'retreat' was because of the "feminist lobby."

We had not seen the last of Senator Anne Cools, antifeminist and media darling. In March, 2000, when B.C. resident Darrin White hung himself, the media reported that according to a certain Liberal Senator he "might well be alive today if Justice Minister Anne McLellan had adopted reforms intended to reduce divisive conflicts between parents involved in bitter divorces."[16] White was reportedly "suicidal" because the courts ordered him to pay more in child support than he was earning while he was on long term disability. Ergo, the courts, the Justice Minister, and of course his ex-wife, were responsible for his suicide.

Cools has been quoted regarding the "increasing politicization" of the judiciary;[17] she told pro-lifers at an anti-abortion conference that parliament should revisit the issue of abortion,[18] and she called on Canadians to protest the fact that "70 percent of mothers win sole custody of their children after a divorce.[19] Cools was quoted about a private member's Bill which would jail convicted murderers for longer time periods,[20] and about the unfairness to gun owners of gun control legislation.[21] In a *National Post* article about "the end of the women's movement," she was quoted as saying, "What has become clear is that whatever it is that gender feminists are advocating, the public has no appetite for it. The public has no more appetite for political correctness or tyrannical techniques."[22] Obviously, the media like what she is saying. Incidently, as Susan Faludi has pointed out, there is nothing new about patriarchal predictions of the end of feminism.

> By 1971, the press was calling the women's movement a "fad," a "bore," and "dead"—and taking a rather active roll in hastening the movement's last rights. At *Newsday,* a male editor dispatched a writer on the story with the directive, "Get out there and find an authority who will say this is all a crock of shit."[23]

Cools came to the defence of conservative Alberta justice John McClung in 1999, describing him as a "gracious, sensitive and generous" man, who had been subjected to "a witch hunt."[24] The McClung controversy will receive more attention later. Cools was also quoted on Ontario Bill 117 on domestic violence,[25] and criticizing the federal justice minister in July, 2001.[26]

Senator Cools also has been the subject of feature articles, and columns, coincidentally, in *The National Post* and the Southam press. *The Ottawa Citizen* said, "She delights in challenging militant feminists. Is she antifeminist? 'Not at all. (Broad smile.) I'm an independent woman.' If anything, her track record shows her to believe in an equality of the sexes."[27] Linda Frum began a feature about Cools in *The National Post* in 1998 with an account of the breathing exercises Cools needs to use because of stress brought on by feminists. "I need to reduce my stress. It's these feminists. I don't understand them," Cools said.[28] In a feature on her in *Chatelaine,* strident antifeminist Donna Laframboise approvingly quotes Cools as saying, "This feminism that has grown up suddenly in the last few years, where all virtue and goodness is stacked up on the side of women, and all evil and violence is stacked up on the side of men—well, human nature doesn't work that way."[29]

PSEUDO FEMINISTS

The relationship between Senator Anne Cools and the press may be contextualized within a broader framework of pro-patriarchal spokeswomen, or professional apologists for the status quo, sometimes called: new feminists, post feminists, equity feminists, family feminists, post-ideological feminists, dissenting feminists or just plain pseudo feminists. Notable among these are Katie Roiphe, (*The Morning After*), Camille Paglia (*Sexual Personae*), Christina Hoff Sommers, (*Who Stole Feminism?*), columnist Cathy Young, (*Feminism Without Illusions*), Elizabeth Fox-Genovese (*Feminism is Not the Story of My Life*); former New Republic writer Karen Lehrman, (*The Lipstick Proviso*),[30] Christine Stolba, (*Women's Figures: An Illustrated Guide to the Economic Progress of Women in America*), and Canadians Donna Laframboise, (*The Princess at the Window*), Patricia Pearson, (*When She Was Bad: How and Why Women Get Away With Murder*), Danielle Crittenden (*What Our Mothers Didn't Tell Us*), and Kate Fillion (*Lip Service*).

Just to take the example of Donna Laframboise, she has written for *The Toronto Star*, *The Globe and Mail*, Southam newspapers, and now *The National Post*. Here are some of her recent articles and columns: *The National Post*: "Domestic violence isn't a gender issue," July 18, 2001; "Save us from social workers on crusade," July 12, 2001; "End the breast cancer hype," June 27, 2001; "When dad becomes a dirty word," June 14, 2001; (lead: "Just when I think it's not possible to feel any more depressed about modern feminism, along comes another reason to slit my wrists;") "Don't censor this porn—please," June 7, 2001; "In the name of the father," May 31, 2001; "Unwanted advances: New research from the University of Guelph concludes that the role of sexual predator is no longer the domain of men," December 8, 1998; "Sheltered from reality: For too long, says an authority on violence against women, society has ignored the fact that women can be violent, too," November 23, 1998; *The Globe and Mail*: "FEMINISM: You've come a long way, baby...And for what? Most women love their husbands, fathers, brothers and sons. No wonder they feel little attachment to a women's movement that is plagued by anti-male hostility, intolerance and extremism," July 26, 1997; "Roll back the red carpet for boys: How come when girls fail it's society's doing, but when boys fail it's their fault?" March 7, 1998; "Who's the victim now? In our outrage over sex crimes, the rights of the accused are sometimes overlooked by the media and the public. The sordid saga of the Grandview Training School abuse trials is a case in point," November 8, 1997; *The Montreal Gazette*: "Author challenges feminism to update for 'the real world,'" July 19, 1997; "You must remember this: Author betrays own criteria in study of recovered memory," February 15, 1997; *The Ottawa Citizen*: "Sex case double standard," June 20, 1997; and *The Edmonton Journal*: "Police 'negligent;' judge awards rape victim $220,000," July 4, 1998.

In each of these articles and others, Laframboise demonstrates her antifeminist bias. For example, in the last article cited, Laframboise chose to interview just one person for her story about a court decision awarding damages to a woman who was raped. The police failed to notify the public about the so-called "balcony rapist," after four rape attacks. "Jane Doe" became his fifth victim. Laframboise interviewed Professor Robert Martin, who teaches law at the University of Western Ontario, who said,

> [T]here should be an appeal and a complaint to the judicial council. He saw no evidence the woman's rights had been violated. "I believe in the integrity of our justice system and I find it utterly unacceptable that judges make judgments which are entirely statements of ideology and have nothing to do with the facts and nothing to do with the law. It is not the function of judges to address and correct all of society's ills...or to enforce bizarre ideological conceptions on society."

Laframboise did also summarize something Jane Doe had said, without using a direct quote: "Doe said it was gratifying to see the judge incorporate the same feminist language she herself has used." In doing this, and in mentioning an award Jane Doe was given by the NAC, Laframboise was labelling Doe and the woman judge in the case as feminists, in an attempt to discredit the decision, with which she obviously disagreed. At Southam, this passed for an objective report on a court decision. Eventually, the Toronto police services board decided not to appeal the decision, despite professor Martin's free advice, and a year later the Toronto police enlisted Jane Doe's help in drafting guidelines for warning the public when serial killers and rapists are on the loose.[31]

Laframboise and these other antifeminists have the direct or indirect support of the corporate patriarchy, in return for furthering its cause of keeping women in their place. They are hired guns. One example is the employment provided to Laframboise and Patricia Pearson by *The National Post*, in return for their regular antifeminist rants, and in recognition of their books, which are favourably reviewed and touted in feature articles. Here's how Michele Landsberg of *The Toronto Star* summed things up in 1997, pre-*Post*:

> [N]ow is the time (just like the 1950s, come to think of it) when female freelance writers are falling over themselves to proclaim their loyalty to dads, male dominance, the patriarchy and all the piercing gender insights of, say, a Popeye or a Preston Manning. Why has their shining hour come round again? Why can't we shake any neo-con mag or rag without their flaky prose showering out like so much dandruff? Let me put it this way. Why do auto workers all want to work for Ford, Chrysler and General Motors? Because that's who owns the factories and pays the wages. *Why are the backlash babes now so ubiquitous? Because conservative ideologues own most of the media, and they're eager to promote any feminist-bashing, no matter how illogical, stale or under researched, so long as it's by a female scribbler—and preferably one who perversely calls herself a feminist.*[32]

Of course, the antifeminist message is overwhelming but not monolithic. The occasional column or letter from a feminist perspective makes it into the neo-con press. And occasionally, the antifeminists go too far even for their own kind. Danielle Crittenden's book, for example, was so bad that even Laframboise couldn't stomach it. As another critical reviewer wrote in *The Globe and Mail*,

> *What Our Mothers Didn't Tell Us* circuitously embroiders the follow-
> ing thesis: In spite of what feminists say, "We want to marry hus-
> bands who will love and respect us; we want to have children; we
> want to be good mothers." Women who do not want this are dis-
> missed: They are lesbians (who, when mentioned at all, are associ-
> ated with cat-fanciers and women with "odd personalities") or
> "crazed" radical feminists who are "pretending [they are] the same
> as men."[33]

Even so, most of the reaction to Crittenden has been positive. CNN made her a regular panellist on *Take 5*. *The Wall Street Journal* was so taken with her that they published her serialized novel, Amanda.Bright@Home, on line. Here's an excerpt from Chapter 11, published in July, 2001. Amanda's husband Bob has just woken her, holding a copy of the morning paper, with the results of an interview Amanda gave to a gossip columnist the previous day.

> "Jesus, Amanda." Bob sat down on the opposite corner of the bed, as
> far away from her, she felt, as it was as possible for him to be without
> leaving the room. His face appeared torn between anger and an al-
> most childish look of betrayal. He gazed into the armchair where yes-
> terday's flotsam of shirts, socks and pants had collected, his robe
> hanging limply on him as if his whole being had suddenly become in-
> animate, like a suit valet or bathroom hook. Amanda knew instinc-
> tively that she must say something, and she wished to console him, to
> apologize, to convince him that there had been a terrible misunder-
> standing. But he had never seemed so remote from her, and Amanda
> feared that uttering even a gentle word might alienate him further.
> Instead, she stared helplessly at him, praying he would turn to her,
> praying he would pat her leg under the sheet, praying he would
> break this wall of glass between them.[34]

Perhaps that should be "Amanda-not-so-bright@Home"—staring helplessly, praying silently, desperately seeking approval and forgiveness.

Crittenden's partner isn't named Bob, he is David, the celebrated ultra conservative David Frum, a *National Post* columnist, speech writer for President George W. Bush, author of *Dead Right* and *What's Right*, and fellow of the conservative *Manhattan Institute* (*MI*) in New York. The *MI* is devoted to "free-market economics, conservative values and the dismantling of the welfare state," says *The Boston Globe.*[35] *MI* president Lawrence J. Mone, writes candidly on their website:

> "[Our senior fellows'] provocative books, reviews, interviews, speeches, articles, and op-ed pieces have been the main vehicle for communicating our message. Books are central to our approach. *We make every effort to ensure that our authors are published by respected trade publishers and that their books receive as much review attention and publicity as possible. Nothing allows us to make a sustained, comprehensive argument more effectively.*"

Danielle Crittenden was founding Editor of *The Women's Quarterly*, which is sponsored by the *Independent Women's Forum*, (IWF) a "non-profit, non-partisan organization" in Washington, D.C. The IWF in turn is sponsored by the right-wing *American Enterprise Institute* (AEI). One of the senior fellows at the AEI, aside from Newt Gingrich, is Christina Hoff Sommers, who is also the "chairman" of the *Independent Women's Forum*. According to its web page, the AEI is "dedicated to preserving and strengthening the foundations of freedom—limited government, private enterprise, vital cultural and political institutions, and a strong foreign policy and national defense." The AEI was Established in 1943 to develop what it said were "...*the types of studies that would be useful in advancing business positions* in public-policy debates."[36]

An example of the way it does this comes from *Media Transparency*, which lists grants received by the AEI, and their sources. Included is a grant for $50,000 provided on January 1, 1999, by the Olin Foundation, for

"Completion of a book, *Pride or Prejudice: Do Women Need Affirmative Action?* by Diana Furchtgott-Roth and Christine Stolba."[37] *Media Transparency* has listed $24.5 million (U.S.) in grants received by the right-wing institute Accuracy In Media (AIM) between 1985 and 1999, mostly from conservative foundations and corporations.[38]

The Women's Quarterly tell us on its web site that it offers "an intelligent refutation of the leading feminist nonsense that is swallowed so uncritically by the mainstream press." One of the ways its sponsor, the *Independent Women's Forum* offers refutation is through the "campus project," which provides "information, guidance, and support for students seeking an alternative to the rigid feminist orthodoxy that is part of today's campus atmosphere." And one of the ways they do this is by running ads in college newspapers, exhorting women to "Take Back the Campus!" The IWF lists what it calls the ten most common myths purveyed by the "cult of campus feminism." And advises, "if you believe two or more of these untruths, you may need deprogramming." The IWF provides what it says is a rebuttal, and then encourages students to snitch on professors who espouse these myths in their classes, so the IWF can "print it on our campus website, SheThinks.org," and send a correction to the professor. (Reprinted in Appendix A.)

THE MORNING AFTER

Katie Roiphe was a Harvard graduate and 25-year-old graduate student in English at Princeton when she wrote *The Morning After: Sex, Fear and Feminism on Campus*, in 1993. Roiphe argued that sexual violence is anomalous, and appearances to the contrary can be explained away as a kind of mass hysteria, fomented by "man-hating fanatics."[39] Research for the book was largely based on her personal experiences and those of her close friends; her review of the academic literature was largely restricted to a 1985 article in *Ms.* magazine.

Roiphe never reviews the statistics on rape, never interviews any rape researchers, never talks to a single woman who has been raped.

The only 'evidence' she marshals to disprove the statistic that one in four college women experience a rape or an attempted rape is her astonishing remark that, as far as she knows, none of her college girlfriends has ever been raped.[40]

Of course, the U.S. media loved the book, which received a cover story in *Time* magazine, a favourable cover story review in *The New York Times Review of Books*, glowing articles in *The Times*, et cetera. One of the very few negative reviews was published by Pollitt in *The New Yorker*.

Sometimes she dismisses the problems as inconsequential: coerced intercourse is bad sex, widespread sexual violence a myth. Sometimes she suggests that the problem is real, but is women's fault: they should be more feisty and vociferous...Sometimes she argues the women's movement has been so successful in moving women into the professions that today's feminists are whining about nothing. And sometimes she argues that men, if seriously challenged to change their ways and habits, will respond with a backlash.[41]

Roiphe indicated that she was "date raped" several times herself, with no untoward consequences. Later, in a 1997 essay in *Esquire*, Roiphe confessed to "forbidden" fantasies about being "taken care of" by a man of means. In traditional sex roles, she writes, "you can take a rest from yourself...equality is not always, in all contexts and situations, comfortable or even desirable."[42]

Her second book, *Night In Paradise: Sex and Morals at the Century's End*, was a confused and meandering treatment of sexual freedom and AIDS (which her sister contracted). No clear feminist targets here. Panned in reviews, she has largely dropped from the media radar. Roiphe's novel *Still She Haunts Me*, inspired by Charles Dodgson (Lewis Carroll) and Alice Liddell, is due to be released in September, 2001. At last, she has begun to formally write fiction. Meanwhile, numerous others have taken her place, such as Christina Hoff Sommers, and Danielle Crittenden.

Christina Sommers was hailed in *The Boston Globe's* headlines as "A Rebel in the Sisterhood," who "Wants to Rescue Feminism from its 'Hijackers.'" As Susan Faludi points out, "It would be more accurate to describe this drama as a media-assisted invasion of the body of the women's movement: the Invasion of the Feminist Snatchers."[43] Hoff Sommers has written that "clever and powerful feminists" who are backed by "well-funded, prestigious organizations as well as individuals," are tricking women into believing that such a thing as the patriarchy still exists.[44] That same patriarchy which provided Hoff Sommers with a grant for $15,000 for "research assistance," from the AEI via the Olin Foundation, on January 1, 1997.[45]

Faludi notes that in their rush to broadcast the views of these faux feminists, the media have not stopped to examine their credentials. If they did, "they wouldn't find these women out on the hustings, in the streets, guarding a family planning clinic from anti-abortionist attacks, or lending a hand at a battered women's shelter."

> They do no writing, speaking, organizing, or activism on behalf of women's equality at all... A review of their published writings unearths not one example of a profeminist article or book...They define themselves as feminists, but their dismissive, to outright hostile, attitudes toward feminist issues—from sexual harassment to domestic violence to rape to pay equity to child care to welfare rights—locate them firmly on the antifeminist side of the ledger.[46]

What these have in common, Faludi points out, is their view that feminism has gone far enough—in fact it's gone much too far, so women should now stop pushing for their own rights and start defending men's rights instead. Instead of rising through academia, these writers have come to us from conservative antifeminist journals such as *National Review*, and *Commentary*, and *The New Republic*.

Here's how Faludi sums up their views:

> Their position, boiled down to its essentials, is that feminism is obsolete, that women are not victims of anything, that it's insulting to

think of women as victims at all, and that everything women do (particularly if it is sexual) is empowering. Since women are such strong, liberated, free agents in today's world, they argue, if bad things happen to women it must be their own fault. Date rape? She should have known better than to go out with that jerk. Stranger rape? She should have been smarter than to travel without a gun. Where a radical feminist would see exploitation and oppression in a topless bar, the "new feminists" see modern goddesses flaunting their sexual power over men.[47]

DISTORTING RESEARCH

In many ways, the October 23, 1999 edition of *The Windsor Star* was a classic. The first thing to grab your attention was the huge colour photo of U.S. Secretary of State Madeleine Albright, playing an African drum, surrounded by grinning Nairobi tribesmen and women, decked out in colourful costumes. Aren't those visible minorities cute and quaint, doing their thing?

On either side of the photo there were economic stories. To the right, a story which took to task Federal finance minister Paul Martin for being too slow with the tax cuts demanded by the media for months on end. To the left, a story about how Ontario hospitals, desperate for cash, are topping up OHIP payments to MDs. Just another example of the crisis in health care. When will privatization rescue us from this morass?

At the bottom of the page, a 'SPECIAL REPORT' about bitterness over the recent CAW contracts which are the envy of everyone, including professionals such as professors, teachers and nurses, and casino workers. Fat cat auto workers.

But the absolute worst story of the entire lot on that pathetic day of jaundiced journalism was the one headlined, "Feminism Leaves Girls Angry, Confused." It was quite similar to the same day story in *The Vancouver Sun*, headlined, "Feminism Driving Some Violent Girls, Researchers Say." Now Conrad Black's Southam Newspapers, including *The Windsor Star*, were blatantly distorting the results of academic research in order to blame the feminist movement for violence and anger in young women.

FEMINISM LEAVES GIRLS ANGRY, CONFUSED

by Louise Surette, Southam News
TORONTO—The feminist movement has left many young girls with confusing messages about how to act and, as a result, a growing number are turning violent, experts say.

Southam Inc. falsely represented the results of a qualitative study by researchers at Toronto's Earlscourt Child and Family Centre, which found increasing anger and violence among some young girls from 16 families who were attending an anger-management program. Southam splashed the story on front pages across the country that day. In the story, Southam blamed "feminism" for allegedly "confusing" young girls about how to act, resulting in violence. According to the news reports, the majority of the girls, aged six to 12, "reported physical or psychological trauma at an early age, leading to violent behaviour." Southam reported that "the number [of girls] in treatment has doubled to one girl for every two boys," and that many of the girls had very poor relationships with their mothers, just as their mothers had with their own mothers.

Somehow, Southam writer Louise Surette and Southam editors managed to turn this evidence into an indictment of feminism. Coincidence? One of the psychologists who participated in the study, Kirsten Madsen, was horrified when she was told about the way Southam portrayed their research.

"We didn't say anything about feminism being responsible. We didn't mention feminism at all," Madsen said in an interview. The researchers did not find, as reported, that there is an increase in violence and aggression by young women, Madsen said. She said the study was a qualitative analysis, and there was no attempt to generalize to the population at large.

Barbara Black, Conrad Black's wife and the Vice President responsible for Editorial Policy at Southam News at the time, has ardently opposed feminism for decades, as has her husband. In 1980 Amiel wrote, "There is a tiny hysterical band of militants in the fringe of the Women's Movement. . .[a] little fringe of libbers [which] has gone a long way toward institutionalizing the perverse minority views of radical feminism in our society." In her column in *Maclean's* Magazine, Amiel Black has written about feminism as the "WoMovement," which, she writes, "is a frankly Marxist-inspired movement."[48]

The story took a relatively innocuous quote from Debra Pepler, director of the LaMarsh Centre for Research on Violence at York University, and juxtaposed the quote with the exaggerated research findings, to fabricate a case against feminism. Pepler referred to the important advances in women's liberation, and then said we have failed to help girls to understand how to be equal without relying on negative male stereotypes of fighting and aggression. To the antifeminists at Southam, this was easily transformed into an attack on feminism, although the researchers, including Pepler, disavow any such connection.

'NOXIOUS REPORTING'

The director of the research centre where the study on aggression and young girls was conducted said later in an interview that the Southam news report on their study was "so seriously skewed" that she found it "hard to imagine how to respond." Dr. Kathy Levene of Toronto's Earlscourt Child and Family Centre said she wrote to Southam newspapers to complain about the story, which she described as "noxious reporting."

"Headlining feminism as a contributing factor to girlhood aggression is a real disservice to the Symposium and, by extension, to the community which is receiving this form of sensational, biased reporting," Dr. Levene commented. "The use of 'hot', melodramatic phrases such as "families whose lives have been torn apart by angry daughters" and "torn apart by the uncontrollable anger of their daughters" perpetuates a victimization theme that indeed is a distortion," Dr. Levene said. Dr. Levene, the clinical director at Earlscourt, where the study was conducted, wrote to Southam newspapers complaining that, "Your sensational headline blaming feminism for the ills of young aggressive girls was not borne out by the article and certainly not by the Symposium on Girlhood Aggression. No presenter linked it to the development of violent girls."

Insight into the corporate media portrayal of violence and feminism comes from alternative media writer Nicole Nolan, who says the question of increasing female violence dates to the mid-1990s and Karla Homolka's partnership in crime with Paul Bernardo.[49]

When Reena Virk was murdered in November, 1997 in Victoria B.C., allegedly by several teenaged girls and one boy, violence by young girls leapt onto the national agenda, from *Maclean's* magazine, to CBC *Newsworld's Benmergui Live*, to *The Globe and Mail*. By the time five 15-year-old Toronto school girls were arrested on charges of extortion in January, 1998, *Globe and Mail* reporter Isabel Vincent concluded that what we were dealing with was "a cross-Canada crime wave of escalating violence by teenaged girls." *The Toronto Star* said, "Violence on Rise Among Girls," and "Girls growing more violent, aggressive."[50]

Some writers, such as conservative Ted writing in *The Financial Post*, said that the violence could be attributed to a laissez-faire, child-centred education system, a government bureaucracy of social workers who take children out of their homes because of the mere allegation of sexual abuse, children of immigrants—"a people largely amputated from their cultural past, drifting about, undirected by any rooted system of values, a sociological time bomb;" as well as "rock videos, superstar musicians with frankly diabolical messages, violent television, sexual experimentation, teen gangs, booze and pot."[51]

But one tack taken in the press was to blame women themselves and feminism.

Although it's tempting to dismiss this coverage as merely another instance of media sensationalism, Nolan argues that the hysteria should be taken seriously.

In the aftermath of the Virk murder, commentators and journalists have not only sensationalised girl violence, they've made some sweeping generalizations about all young women. Following long-standing misogynist traditions, they've made the assumption that the behaviour of a few reveals the brutality of all girls and that increased freedom for women—brought about specifically by feminism—is responsible for the supposed rise in young women's violence.

Although some of the discussion around Reena Virk's murder was sane and informative, to understand the issues we have to examine the way violent and aggressive females have been used "to justify control of—and even violence against—women," and how they function as a justification for increasing social controls on women and girls, Nolan says. One of Canada's prominent criminologists, Anthony Doob of the University of Toronto, recently wrote in the *Canadian Journal of Criminology*, condemning media assertions of increasing and worsening girl violence. "There is no evidence whatsoever of increases in the most serious kind of violence," wrote Doob. The apparent increase in minor assaults is more likely due to a less tolerant view of youth violence, reflected by policy changes such as Ontario's "zero-tolerance" approach to violence and crime.

"We're seeing an increased focus on behaviour that used to be ignored or rationalized away in other ways. Girls fighting, taunting and teasing is not a new phenomenon. What's new is to have it result in charges of assault," says Kim Pate, executive director of the Canadian Association of Elizabeth Fry Societies. What makes girl violence such an urgent topic is this not-so-hidden agenda of attributing these incidents to the core character of women generally. The most visible proponent of this argument is antifeminist Patricia Pearson, whose book, *When She was Bad* (subtitled *Violent Women and the Myth of Innocence*) hit bookstores in fall, 1997. *The Toronto Star* reviewer wondered aloud why Pearson, then a contributing editor at Conrad Black's *Saturday Night* magazine, "would devote an entire book to the depiction of women as cowardly, irresponsible, malicious, vengeful, cold-blooded, sometimes psychotic child molesters and/or murderers, spouse batterers, predators and serial killers?"[52]

The Virk murder, Pearson wrote in *The Globe and Mail*, "has shattered our illusions about the gentler sex." She counselled readers to imagine satchel-carrying schoolgirls "beating one another to death." The angelic image of women which Pearson says must be eradicated, according to Nolan is actually a limited view when compared with the prevailing historical and contemporary pictures of women as irrational, impulsive, and socially and politically inferior. Historically, alleged aggression in women has provided an excuse for rigorous social control.

After a 17-year-old girl assaulted another girl in Kitchener, Ontario, in January 1998, *The Globe and Mail* ran the front page headline, "Teen's Torture Again Reveals Girls' Brutality," in a "generalization that surely would never be tolerated if it referred to a racial minority or any other group," writes Nolan.[53] The first paragraph in this story read as follows: "The 'horrifying' torture and beating of a teenager in Kitchener, Ont., on the weekend is yet another example of what law-enforcement officials and experts say is an alarming wave of violent crimes by girls across Canada." The victim had her hair "hacked off with a knife," and was beaten to the point where "her eyes are swollen shut," according to *The Globe*. The reporter then went on to quote Patricia Pearson:

> "There's no question that violent crimes by girls are on the increase," said Patricia Pearson, a journalist and author of *When She Was Bad*, a recently published study of female violence. "Girls have been doing this with increasing frequency over the last five years, probably because there is an increase in their comfort level with the use of weapons and a sense of empowerment with tactics that have been traditionally dominated by males."[54]

This last reference is clearly code for feminist values. Aside from the obvious manipulation of statistics, one of the remarkable features of the "girl crime" hysteria has been the way that women's increasing freedom has been blamed for increased violence, says Nolan. Feminism has long been used as a scapegoat for violence and aggression in children. Typically, it has been tied into child neglect by working mothers, but now, "instead of being blamed for indirectly victimizing youth, [feminism] has been cast in the more active role of actually urging them on to greater acts of evil. Having freed girls from the repressive ways of the past, feminism, the theory goes, has also freed their aggressive natures," says Nolan. This is exactly what is being blamed, without an iota of evidence, in the recent Southam news story.

Why are girls acting out? Patricia Pearson asked and answered, "Probably because girls are thinking: it's okay now, if you're female, to be demonstrably angry. It's okay to express yourself forcefully." Nolan says feminism:

> ...is part of the cultural atmosphere, and teenage girls, like the rest of us, absorb its influence. That it causes confusion when it collides with other ideas about gender roles is understandable. But to believe that increased freedom associated with feminism causes girls' violence is to believe—much like the misogynists of the European tradition [of the 16th and 17th centuries]—that women have volatile natures that can only be held in check by restrictive social controls.[55]

While the theory that feminism will lead to more violence has been a fiercely debated subject in criminology circles since the 1970s, there has been no link between feminism and violent crime. In fact, says Nolan, "there is plenty of evidence to indicate just the opposite."

"Even those who believe girls' violence is on the rise have rejected the connection between feminism and girls' violence...[in] her book *Sex, Power and the Violent School Girl*, University of Victoria professor Sibylle Artz concluded that women were given even less value than usual in violent girls' homes." [56] Artz's research also showed that violent girls have more conservative gender and sexual mores. Violent girls come from blue-collar, two-parent families that are rigidly hierarchical: the father bullying, mother placating. Alcohol misuse and violent interaction are typical. The girls have endured physical and sexual abuse, according to Artz.

American criminologist Meda Chesney-Lind says, "almost all of the existing criminological literature stresses the role played by discrimination and poverty...in the creation of crime," rather than "feminism," which improves girls and women's economic conditions.[57] Nolan says it's a short jump from the thesis that freedom makes girls violent, to the conclusion that the key to stopping this "dangerous trend" is to restrict them once again. "The rhetoric of panicked urgency surrounding this supposedly 'sharply rising' girl violence favours quick solutions over progressive ones—the punitive over the therapeutic."

"Many prosecutors and social scientists," advised *Maclean's*, "caution against easier treatment for girls than boys." In the same article, Halifax Crown attorney Catherine Cogswell remarked that the system should not deal "with girls with kid gloves." According to Nolan, "this issue needs attention—but the right kind. Those who have spent a lot of time thinking about severely violent girls tend to believe that exploring the girls' own experience—including factors such as sexual abuse, poverty, race and class—is a more useful long-term solution than reforming the Young Offenders Act or giving girls stiffer punishments."

Blaming feminism for an alleged increase in aggression and violence amongst girls is one blatant aspect of the backlash against feminism.

DIVORCED WOMEN 'ANGRIEST'

Less than two weeks after running the story about feminism making women violent, *The National Post* was back at it again, this time distorting research in order to claim that divorced women are the angriest group in society. Dr. Scott Schieman, a sociologist at the University of Miami said in an interview that he was upset and somewhat bewildered by a report on his research which ran in *The National Post* in November, 1999. *The Post* distorted and fabricated findings from Schieman's research, which was published in the then-current issue of *The Journal of Health and Social Behavior*. The *Post*'s article, by Paul Waldie, said, "Divorced women in their 30s are the most irate."

But Dr. Schieman said he told Mr. Waldie in an interview that he found no gender differences of any sort in his study, which was about age differences in anger levels. "I didn't even find sex differences. The headline is nuts," said an irate Dr. Schieman. The lead paragraph in Waldie's story read, "Divorced women in their 30s who are unemployed and don't go to church are among the angriest people around, according to a new study, while elderly widowers who attend church regularly are the most even-tempered." But Dr. Schieman said he told *The Post* that while some research has found gender differences in reported anger, his study did not support that finding. What's more, his U.S. sample, which was a representative random sample, didn't demonstrate any differences between divorced and married respondents.

"There were some differences with marital status in the Canadian sample, which was not a representative sample," Dr. Schieman said. "I made no attempt to generalize from it." Near the end, *The National Post* story did say that, "As for the sexes, Dr. Schieman said his study was not conclusive, but two recent studies have shown 'that women report significantly higher levels of anger than men.'"

"This is upsetting. I never made such sweeping claims in my findings," Dr. Schieman said. In his article he studied a sample of 951 "physically disabled" people in southern Ontario who were interviewed in 1981, as well as a national sample of about 1,450 Americans who were interviewed in 1996. *The National Post* article implied that both samples were representative, and said the studies "drew remarkably similar conclusions about who is angry and why." Dr. Schieman did find that "people who were more involved in religious activities" showed less measurable anger, but to translate that into an elderly widower who goes to church is simplistic and wrong.

"What they [say they] have extracted from my study is nowhere to be found in my study," he said. Dr. Schieman said, "I shrieked when I saw what they had done. I called in other people to show them" *The National Post* web site, on his office computer.

The National Post story is fraught with errors and misrepresentations about the published research. "They said I reported that senior managers are more angry. I didn't study that," Dr. Schieman said.

Contacted at *The National Post*, Mr. Waldie said that he believes he reported fairly on the study, "based on what Dr. Schieman told me." Waldie said the story had been changed "a little bit" by editors, from what he wrote. Asked about the first paragraph, Waldie said he reported Dr. Schieman's words about "what other studies had found," even if they weren't his own findings. Yet, the lead makes explicit reference to the results of "a new study." Asked if he thought it was misleading, if people would get the impression that Dr. Schieman's research had found gender differences, based on the first paragraph of his story, Mr. Waldie said, "No. But I can see where you think it's misleading." When informed that Dr. Schieman was upset about the way *The National Post* reported his research, Mr. Waldie said, "He can't be that upset. I haven't heard from him."

Somehow, *The National Post* managed to turn Dr. Scott Schieman's study on age differences in an American sample, into one about "angry divorced women" in their 30s in both Canada and the U.S., all of which was fabricated in accord with the anti-feminist agenda of *The Post*.

NOTES

1. Chuck Sinkevitch, "Her path became 'a death spiral': Tragic ending to a 'crazy life,' *The Windsor Star*, October 11, 1994, p.A1.

2. Canadian Press, "Cools blames moms for male violence: Women's Day meeting ends in anger," *The Globe and Mail*, March 8, 1995, p.A1.

3. Cited in Michele Landsberg, "Custody committee leaves trail of toxic myths," *The Toronto Star*, November 14, 1998.

4. Laura Flanders, "Campus Feminists: The Media's New Bogeywomen," *Extra!*, March/April 1994. http://www.fair.org/extra/9403/campus-feminists.html

5. Anne Cools, "Reflections of a Black Canadian senator," *Calgary Herald*, March 24, 2001.

6. Margaret Philp, "Statistics don't back Cools' abusive-mothers charge," *The Globe and Mail*, March 9, 1995.

7. Margaret Philp, "Senator hits back at critics of her child-abuse statements: Cools blames 'feminist ideologues' for obscuring women's role in domestic violence, but authors say she is pushing their data too far,"*The Globe and Mail*, April 4, 1995.

8. Susanne Hiller, "The crime few believe a mother can commit," *The Halifax Daily News*, January 19, 1997.

9. Margaret Wente, "Anne Cools, renegade," *The Globe and Mail*, March 1, 1997.

10. There are dozens of examples. For just one more, see Margaret Wente, "Counterpoint: Gender Science at MIT," *The Globe and Mail,* December 16, 1999.

11. Cf. Jennifer Pozner, "Women Have Not Taken Over the News: TV Guide should look at the numbers before they cheer journalistic gender parity," *Extra!*, Fairness and Accuracy In Reporting, January/February 2000.
http://www.fair.org/extra/0001/tvguide.html

12. For another example, see Ezra Levant, "Only left-wing lesbians need apply," *The National Post*, January 5, 2000.

13. Michele Landsberg, "Child access report useless mish-mash," *The Toronto Star*, December 13, 1998.

14. Michele Landsberg, "Custody committee leaves trail of toxic myths," *The Toronto Star*, November 14, 1998.

15. Bestdigest.com claims that *Mrs. Doubtfire* (which is a touching film) is the top-grossing Robin Williams film ever, at $219 million.

16. Jeff Lee, "Senator says conflict reforms might have saved father's life: Anne Cools says a committee identified ways of reducing divisive conflicts between parents," *The Vancouver Sun*, March 24, 2000.

17. Neil Seeman, "Who runs Canada?: The tug of war between Parliament and the Supreme Court is becoming thornier as judges become more openly political, observers contend," *The National Post*, July 24, 1999.

18. Carmelina Prete, "Senator encourages support for pro-lifers," *The Hamilton Spectator*, July 4, 1998.

19. Rachel Brighton, "Custody not awarded fairly, says Senator," *The Halifax Daily News*, April 27, 1998.

20. Norm Ovenden, "Tough sentencing bill could be killed in Senate: Cools: Popular legislation would jail multiple murderers longer," *The National Post*, June 22, 1999.

21. Donna Laframboise, "Hurricane Anne," *Chatelaine*, August, 1997, pp. 32-37.

22. Quoted in Luiza Chwialkowska, The end of the women's movement, *The National Post*, November 28, 1998.

23. Susan Faludi, "I'm Not a Feminist But I Play One on TV," *Ms.* Magazine, March/April, 1995. http://www.mtsu.edu/~jaeller/faludi

24. Shawn Ohler, "Groundswell of support rises for embattled McClung: Respected by lawyers: Supporters fear witch hunt against 'gracious' judge," *The National Post*, March 3, 1999.

25. See Dave Brown, "Men 'one phone call' from total destruction': Accused abusers would lose freedom, property under Bill 117," *The Ottawa Citizen*, November 4, 2000; Dave Brown, "Bill 117 guts men's rights," *The Ottawa Citizen*, December 20, 2000. Brown, senior editor at *The Citizen*, would appear to be a fervent men's rights advocate.

26. Robert Fife, "Liberals assail minister's lawmaking: McLellan accused of undemocratic tactics with child custody bill," *The National Post*, July 26, 2001.

27. Dave Brown, "Senator Answers Child's Call for Help," *The Ottawa Citizen*, March 18, 2000.

28. Linda Frum, "Anne Cools' absence of malice: Outspoken senator says she doesn't take sides on the family," *The National Post*, December 19, 1998.

29. Laframboise, "Hurricane Anne."

30. For an account of and response to *The Lipstick Proviso*, see Susan Faludi, "Revisionist Feminism," letter to Karen Lehrman, Dialogue, *Slate* Archives, April 28, 1997. http://slate.msn.com/Dialogues/97-04-30/Dialogues.asp?iMsg=1

31. Scot Magnish "Victim Helped Cops Set Guidelines," *The Toronto Sun*, October 20, 1999.

32. Michele Landsberg, "Backlash babes turn back clock on feminism," *The Toronto Star*, September 13, 1997. (Emphasis added)

33. Lynn Crosbie, "Agitprop for 'real' women," *The Globe and Mail*, February 20, 1999.

34. http://opinionjournal.com/columnists/dcrittenden/

35. Harvey Robins, "Conservatives plant a seed in NYC," *The Boston Globe*, February 22, 1998.

36. Quoted in Media Transparency, The Money Behind the Media, (emphasis added). http://www.mediatransparency.org/recipients/aei.htm

37. http://www.mediatransparency.org/search_results/info_on_any_recipient.asp?19

38. Available through the Media Transparency web site at www.mediatransparency.org, or http://www.mediatransparency.org/search_results/info_on_any_recipient.asp?19

39. Taken from Katha Pollitt, "Not Just Bad Sex," review of Roiphe's book in *The New Yorker*, Vol. 69, No 32, pp. 220-224, 10/4/93. http://www.interactivetheatre.org/resc/notbadsex.html

40. Susan Faludi, "I'm Not a Feminist But I Play One on TV," *Ms.* Magazine, March/April, 1995. http://www.mtsu.edu/~jaeller/faludi

41. Pollitt, Not Just Bad Sex.

42. Quoted in Laura Miller, "Sex and the Single Post-Feminist: Bad Girl Katie Roiphe Used to Be Disgusted. Now She's Just Confused," *Salon* Feb 97 http://www.salon.com/feb97/badgirl970226.html

43. Faludi, I'm Not A Feminist.

44. *Ibid.*

45. From Media Transparancy, http://www.mediatransparency.org/search_results/info_on_any_recipient.asp?19

46. Faludi, I'm Not a Feminist.

47. D.A. Clarke, "What is Feminism?" *Feminista!*, Volume 3, Number 10, 2000. http://www.feminista.com/v3n10/clarke.html

48. For these examples and others, see "The Tyranny of Feminism," in Maude Barlow and James Winter, *The Big Black Book: The Essential Views of Conrad and Barbara Amiel Black,* Stoddart, Toronto, 1997.

49. See Nicole Nolan, "Girl Crazy," *This* Magazine 31 (5), March/April, 1998, pp. 31-35. Many of the points in this section come from Nolan's excellent article.

50. Eric Roher, "Girls growing more violent, aggressive," *The Toronto Star*, April 7, 1998; Wendy Cox, "Violence on rise among girls," *The Toronto Star*, December 9, 1997.

51. Cf. Ted Byfield, "Victoria Tragedy Sends up a Flare About Social Systems," *The Financial Post*, November 29, 1997; Ted Byfield, "Heavy-Handed Bureaucrats Don't Know Best in B.C.," *The Financial Post*, April 18, 1998.

52. Kathleen Byrne, "The brutal woman, a victim no more: In the guise of honesty, a gift to the misogynists," *The Toronto-Star*, October 18, 1997.

53. Isabel Vincent, "Teen's torture again reveals girls' brutality: Ontario beating unspeakably violent, terrorized witnesses, police say," *The Globe and Mail*, January 20, 1998.

54. *Ibid.*

55. Nolan, Girl Crazy.

56. Sibylle Artz, *Sex, Power and the Violent School Girl*, Trifolium Books Inc., 1998. Cited in Nolan, Girl Crazy.

57. Meda Chesney-Lind, *Female Gangs in America: Essays on Girls, Gangs, and Gender*, Lake View Press, 1999; also *Girls, Delinquency and Juvenile Justice*, Wadsworth, 2nd Edition, 1997. Cited in Nolan, Girl Crazy.

CHAPTER THREE

THE NUCLEAR DESERT

"Who are they going to attack next, and on what pretext?"
—the Archbishop of San Paulo

Rajmonda Rreci, 18, was a fairly composed interview subject, under the circumstances, when she was first filmed by Nancy Durham of CBC-TV. Rajmonda was identified as an "ethnic Albanian," and her emblematic story was one of persecution, tragedy and injustice. Rajmonda was staying in a makeshift KLA hospital in Shale, run by dedicated volunteers who were also ethnic Albanians, where she was recovering from trauma. Skenderaj, Rajmonda's village, was razed and her tiny six-year-old sister Qendresa had just been killed by the dreaded Kosovo Serbs under Slobodan Milosevic. Rajmonda was in shock, but she was also very angry. From her hospital bed she told Canadian Broadcasting Corporation reporter Nancy Durham that she would take up arms to avenge her sister's death, that she would join the Kosovo Liberation Army (KLA).

Durham's first story was broadcast in September 1998, the second was a documentary titled *Winter of Fear* on CBC TV's National Magazine broadcast in January 1999.[1] A third story followed the next summer. In the second story, Durham continued her theme about the plight of a desperate, persecuted people, with a clear indication of who the villains were.

Durham: "Last summer, several hundred thousand people had fled their homes when their villages came under attack from the Yugoslav army and Serbian police."

Later in the story, she came to "Ramonda's" plight (Durham spelled Rajmonda's name wrong in the first two stories, correcting it in the third), beginning by re-broadcasting file footage from a previous story on Rajmonda, from September 1998.

Durham: "One person I'm looking for is a girl Shpetim introduced me to, Ramonda (sic)."

(File footage) *Dr. Shpetim Robaj:* "She's in stress situation because what's happened to her family, you know."

Durham: "Stressed and angry. When I met Ramonda, (sic) she had just seen her little sister Qendresa killed in the attack on her village."

(September, 1998) *Ramonda* (sic)/ *Patient Turned Kla Soldier:* "And maybe I will be one of the, a part of the Kosovo Liberation Army. Because that's the only way for us—except if the world help us."

This was the end of the file footage: now Durham continued, this time with recent footage.

Durham: "Ramonda (sic) is now a soldier in the Kosovo Liberation Army. [KLA] Dr. Fitim [Selimi] is too, and he's agreed to take me to Ramonda's secret hideout...We travelled by tractor for two hours until we reached the summit and the headquarters of the KLA. Inside a cabin heated by a wood fire, we found two soldiers sleeping by their rifles while six others kept watch. I was forbidden to take pictures—until after a further two hours and as darkness descended, Ramonda (sic) appeared. I was allowed just half an hour with her."

Durham: "Are you in war now or in peace?"

Ramonda: (sic) "We are in war now. But it's something that it's just like killing me inside, because we are in war now. We do everything to get the peace in Kosovo, but other states just, like, don't understand what is the situation here."

Durham: "For Ramonda, (sic) her situation is simple: she saw her little sister die; she witnessed the shelling and burning of her village and she was traumatised. Now this 18-year-old girl has found a way to fight back."

On camera, Rajmonda wielded a rifle.

Ramonda: (sic) "It's a Kalashnikov, and it's just like one member of my family. This is for me everything."
Durham: "Why?"
Ramonda: (sic) "Because he have the power that I don't have it. When we didn't have guns in our hands, they killed us how—just like they wanted. But now we are safer. I have the gun in my hand and if I can't do nothing with them, then I can do with myself, just don't be in their hands. And I'm not going to be in their hands until I have my life." (She begins singing).

After another short narrative, Rajmonda continued.

Ramonda: (sic) "It's so really, really hard. But I am, sometimes I am so lucky that my sister was only seven-years-old, six-years-old, and she had a chance to give her blood for this land. To give her blood for this land. And I promise her and I promise my family and I promise all the peoples, Albanian people, that I will be in war; I will do everything until I die."
Durham: "...Ramonda (sic) too knows the danger, but like so many people here, she is prepared to die."
Ramonda: (sic) "I don't believe that I will be alive when we get the peace, but I don't care. And if I die, I will breathe the breath of freedom—even in this land."
Durham: "For the National, I'm Nancy Durham in Drenica, Kosovo."

THE REAL RAJMONDA

Rajmonda's story was a gripping one, which played around the world on various broadcast networks, in "at least a dozen countries." There was a lot of reaction to this engrossing and heart-rending tale. The only problem with the story about Rajmonda is that it was entirely false.

The real Rajmonda was a KLA member from the outset, when she gave the interview to Durham in the hospital in Shale. The story about her sister's death, the razing of her hometown, her planned conversion to the KLA clause—all false. With the collaboration of medical doctors and staff at the hospital, other KLA members and even her own family, Rajmonda duped veteran CBC reporter Nancy Durham. It was a brilliant and successful piece of propaganda. And, it had resonance: it fit beautifully with what media outlets wanted to hear.

In September, 1999, CBC-TV took the unusual step of airing a 16 minute documentary to explain that significant parts of the earlier documentaries on Kosovo were unfounded. The second documentary, *Winter of Fear*, which aired the previous January, was exceedingly sympathetic to the members of the Kosovo Liberation Army (KLA), and to the 'plight' of the ethnic Albanians generally, at the hands of the Serbs. The new film described how, during a follow-up trip later that summer, after the bombing was over, Durham discovered that Rajmonda was already a KLA soldier when they met in the hospital, and that her sister was still very much alive. It was all orchestrated for propaganda purposes, with the help of the doctors and other KLA members, and family. Durham confronted Rajmonda, who said she lied in part to get on television and help advance the cause of her people. "I said to myself, she is just journalist; she lives in England and she don't care about us. They don't care about us, how we live and how we die. They are coming here just to make interview for their career and for their interests," the highly sophisticated Rajmonda said on camera.

The CBC 'retraction' spent most of the time justifying how Durham could have been fooled, and trying to ascertain why Rajmonda would lie. It made no mention at all of the way the faked documentaries helped to justify the NATO war. Because of course, the overriding assumption was and is that the war was completely justified, regardless of Rajmonda's lies. Even in this third story, the reporter continued to shill, reflexively, for the KLA.

"When we parted that winter night, I had doubts about Rajmonda's ability to survive. Her Kalashnikov rifle was no match for the Yugoslav army. But I had underestimated Rajmonda. In June, I found her still on the mountain. This 19-year-old girl had made it through war," Durham narrated.[2]

When interviewed after the retraction documentary ran, by a *National Post* reporter, Nancy Durham reportedly "bristled," when asked if the network was engaging in a massive correction. "I wouldn't characterize it like that at all," she said. "I don't like having broadcast something that wasn't true, but I stand by what I did one hundred percent."[3] Just what Durham was "standing by" wasn't clear. The lies? Having been duped into supporting the NATO war? Justifying Albanian terrorism?

Kelly Crichton, executive producer of *The National Magazine*, also told *The Post* that the report wasn't a correction. "I certainly think it's setting the record straight on what we said before," she said. "But I think it's trying to go beyond that and trying to analyze why this happened and how it happened and to explore much further the motivation behind Rajmonda doing this." But the CBC was only interested in Rajmonda's personal motivation, as if this were some minor family feud, and not in the bigger picture of the levelling of a country. This 'autopsy of a lie' documentary should have served the purpose of examining all questions afresh, but instead it simply blundered forward under the same constrained ideological blinders, oblivious to the various levels of manipulation.[4]

In the retraction documentary, Nancy Durham narrated: "I had a sinking feeling. Perhaps there never was a Quendresa. Perhaps there was no murdered sister at all. Had I been used for the cause?" At another point she said, the "supposed murder had been the foundation of Rajmonda's story. A story that had played around the world in at least a dozen countries. And each time it was told, it reported Qendresa's death."[5] But that was the extent of it. No discussion of any impact on the war, even though such alleged atrocities were the basis for the NATO bombing. The closest they came was in the following exchange between host Brian Stewart and Durham, in conversation in the studio after playing the retraction documentary.

Stewart: "All the way through the Kosovo war, we had huge demonstrations outside the CBC, the Serb community in Canada claiming that the Western media were being taken in by the KLA and Kosova Liberation Army supporters. Now are they going to say this is Exhibit 'A'—this proves that the Western media was (sic) taken in?"

Durham: "I suppose they will. And I'll have to say yeah, I was taken in by Rajmonda. I believed her. So did others, many others. Yup."

Durham appeared to treat the matter as a personal one, between herself and Rajmonda, and her viewers. She felt badly about being "taken in," and wanted to apologize to the "many others"—her viewers. Not that it would do any good, but it would never dawn on her to apologize to Slobodan Milosevic, or the Serbian people. Durham told Brian Stewart in conversation on CBC's National Magazine,

> [M]any people saw these reports and were moved by them. I think they had a strong impact. I was asked by lots of people 'how is that girl?' 'Have you heard about her?' 'Is she still alive? Did she survive?' It's something to move people like that. If you discovered the foundation of that story is false, I mean there is no question that you have to go back and tell people 'look, I'm sorry.'

Durham couldn't find anyone else who was even *aware* of Rajmonda's lie, let alone responsible for it. Except for Rajmonda's mother, who tried to cover things up by insisting that there was another sister who was killed, and that Rajmonda had gotten her own sister's name wrong. (This was too much to swallow, even for Durham). But Durham did go back to a KLA doctor who earlier acted as her guide, to record his rationalization.

Ilir Tolaj / KLA DOCTOR: "So if this lie—I don't know if it's small or big. Maybe from my point it's small. From the point of the journalist, it's very big and unacceptable. But if this small lie, from my point of view, made some kind of impact on accelerating what West country did in Kosovo, then it's worth [it]."

Like Doctor Tolaj and Rajmonda, Durham is bent on justifying the 'broader truth' behind her story, whatever lies were told. Rajmonda said, "I think about [why I lied] and I said to myself. 'Why I have to tell her my sister is alive when there are so many girls and mothers who lost the childrens, the sisters, the family, they don't have the chance to give interview.' " She continued, "I'm glad it was effective in one [sense], if this was not my story this story belonged to someone else here." For her part, Durham indicated that Rajmonda and her people had to do something, even if it involved subterfuge. "Kosovo was on fire, but the story dominating the news was the Clinton/Lewinsky affair. To many Kosovar Albanians, it seemed the outside world had forgotten them." She concluded,

> The fact is that Rajmonda didn't need a story about a dead sister to explain her motivation. She was born in Drenica in the very place where 18 years later, the war would begin. The first fires of Kosovo's war were set in Prekaz, just a short walk from Rajmonda's home. In March 1998, Serb forces launched an attack against *what they called Albanian terrorists*. It was the assault which alerted the world to the Kosovo conflict. Children were among the 53 members of the Jashari clan who died.

What they called Albanian terrorists. But what if they really were? This is, of course beyond the thinkable. But not for others, operating in the parallel universe outside of *MediaThink*, such as University of Ottawa professor Michel Chossudovsky, and others. Chossudovsky makes a convincing case to this effect. And, as he points out, even U.S. President Bill Clinton's former special envoy for Kosovo told *Agence France Presse* in February 1998 that the KLA "is, without any questions, a terrorist group."[6]

Rajmonda now went on to say that she had a friend who died in *this* assault, and *that* was what drove her into the KLA. This time, Durham is somewhat more sceptical.

Durham: "How do I know that story's true?"
Rajmonda: "Oh you will find it, it's easy."

Durham: "Of course finding the truth here is not at all easy. It's by returning repeatedly to Kosovo that I uncovered Rajmonda's lie. But hers is just one. How many other lies will remain buried?"

How many other lies, indeed. Durham poses a momentous question, but then makes no attempt to answer it.

Under different circumstances repeated errors such as this, from actually getting the interviewee's name wrong, to repeatedly broadcasting serious, fabricated lies without adequate fact-checking, would get a reporter fired or suspended. But that would be for propagating a story which didn't conform to *Mediathink*. Instead, in this instance, because her story resonated so well with the orthodox view on events in Kosovo, CBC-TV and Durham have chosen to venerate her transgressions by *actually entering Durham's 16-minute documentary about her mistakes in film festivals!!!* On the web site about its personalities, the CBC says of Durham,

> Her 1999 film, *The Truth About Rajmonda: A KLA Soldier Lies for the Cause*, investigates why a central figure in her reports from Kosovo persistently lied about her personal history. In March 2000 the film was screened at Sweden's Tempo Documentary Festival in Stockholm, and in Amsterdam at a Dutch public television conference on the impact of new technology on war reporting. In May the film was a topic of discussion in Washington, D.C. at a conference on reporting war crimes, and once more at this year's Edinburgh festival.[7]

Here again, the lies only pertain to Rajmonda's "personal history," and there are no broader ramifications. One would at least hope that at the conference on "the impact of new technology on war reporting," someone would discuss how much more vulnerable "video journalists" such as Durham (who is based in London England) are to this sort of manipulation, when, to save the network money they are sent out alone to research, produce, report, film and record major stories abroad.

During a foreign news roundup at the end of the year, *National Magazine* host Brian Stewart made reference to this aspect of Durham's reporting, but in a positive way. "Nancy Durham represents a new kind of TV reporter. She works solo, doing her own camerawork in the field. She went by herself to Kosovo to profile an Albanian family," he said. On her part, four months had not added much to Durham's perspective. To her, Rajmonda was still acting alone, ("off her own bat," whatever that means) and the lesson was largely a personal one, one of personal trust rather than group ideology.

> I can't honestly say that if I worked there again in a war situation, I wouldn't operate the same way. You go where you can in war and you check in every way you can. But there are great limitations on your ability to move around. But I guess *I have learned that it's very easy to be used, and just by one person acting off their own bat.* I'm not a cynical person and this experience hasn't made me more cynical, but I suppose I have to admit I'm probably a little less trusting.[8]

Contrast this with the broader perspective of Chris Hedges, former *New York Times* Bosnia bureau chief, writing in the journal *Foreign Affairs*, during the bombing of Kosovo. Hedges says, "...the KLA leaders are wary of the outside world and given to secrecy, paranoia, and appalling mendacity when they feel it serves their interests, which is most of the time. The KLA splits down a bizarre ideological divide, with hints of fascism on one side and whiffs of communism on the other."[9] If Durham were to contextualize Rajmonda's lies within the "appalling mendacity" of the KLA leadership, this would be a start. Or, there was Andro Linklater of *The Spectator* in London, on the whole atrocity story hysteria. He could at least recognize, albeit after the fact, that: "Nothing illustrates better the importance of the dispassionate, truth-telling journalist than the mess in the Kosovo campaign, which, it becomes increasingly clear, we were gulled into supporting by manufactured stories of Serb atrocities and refugee suffering."[10]

Or, one could simply put the situation in the FRY into some perspective. Indisputably, the KLA was and is a guerrilla force, with foreign training, funding, supplies and bases, carrying out violent attacks on police and civilians, in order to promote independence. In the process, by the summer of 1998 it had taken control of 40% of Kosovo. Noam Chomsky observes,

> We need scarcely tarry on how the U.S. would respond to attacks by a guerrilla force with foreign bases and supplies, seeking, say, independence for Puerto Rico, or reunification with Mexico of the southwest regions conquered by the expanding North American giant, taking control of 40% of the territory.[11]

Ask yourself: how did the U.S. respond to mere WTO protesters in Seattle, in 1999? Or the Italian police in Genoa in the summer of 2001? How did Jean Chretien react to APEC protesters in Vancouver in 1997? Then-Prime Minister Brian Mulroney called out the army when a handful of Native Canadian protesters threw up a barricade in Oka, Quebec, in 1991. Then-Prime Minister Pierre Trudeau invoked the War Measures Act in response to a handful of FLQ kidnappers in Quebec in 1970. So, whose reaction was extreme?

On March 24, 1999, the day the NATO bombing of Kosovo began, Durham's footage of Rajmonda was also used in another CBC TV news story as an example of the ethnic Albanians who were joining the KLA in response to Serb atrocities: hence as a justification for the bombing.

> *Carol Off:* "...Slowly in frustration, the Kosovo Liberation Army emerged and went on the attack, provoking severe Serbian crackdowns. Each crackdown radicalized more Albanians, who joined the KLA."
>
> *Ramonda* (sic) / KLA SOLDIER: "I will be in war. I will do everything until I die."

Off 'explained' her version (and NATO's) of how we got to this point:

> In the '70s, Belgrade recognized the Albanian majority and gave the province autonomy. Slobodan Milosevic changed all that. Ten years ago, as communism ended, Milosevic unleashed a wave of national-

ism in Yugoslavia. He declared Kosovo the soul of the Serb people and took away its autonomy...As Yugoslavia disintegrated in the 1990s, each region declared independence. First Slovenia and Macedonia, then Croatia went to war for its sovereignty.[12]

KOSOVO: 'A CARICATURE OF REALITY'

The real story of what happened in the Federal Republic of Yugoslavia (FRY, or Serbia and Montenegro) approaches that of East Timor, in terms of tragedy: the horror, the death and destruction, and the wholesale distortion of these events by the media generally. These actions continued into the summer of 2001, with the devastating effects of the international trade sanctions and resultant medicine shortages, just as in Iraq, and the pursuit of the FRY's former president on charges as a war criminal. There was also massive intervention in the internal affairs and elections in FRY by the US government and its agencies, to unseat the Socialist government.

From March 24 to June 3 1999, U.S.-led NATO air forces bombed the FRY, including Kosovo. The bombing destroyed the infrastructure of the FRY, and much of the industrial base of the country, causing an estimated $100 billion in damages. Manufacturing plants and food processing plants were levelled. For 10 weeks, NATO bombed water distribution and purification centres, agricultural centres, historic sites, cultural monuments, hospitals, hotels, museums, and churches. Bus and train depots were reduced to ruins. Major bridges were knocked down, blocking all shipping on the Danube, and polluting that water source beyond repair. Two thousand civilians perished. Electrical generators were destroyed, with no access to replacements. The effects of radioactive air pollution from depleted uranium shells will continue for some time.[13] This was, and remains, an atrocity. According to Yugoslav environmentalists the "humanitarian" bombing of Kosovo may have turned Kosovo into a nuclear desert for future generations there.[14]

You would never know these things by reading most media accounts. A year after the bombing, a news story about war crimes investigations referred simply to: "an 11-week NATO bombing campaign aimed at halting Yugoslav repression of the Albanian inhabitants of the Serb province of Kosovo."[15]

One renowned scholar has termed western media portrayal of these events as "a caricature of reality."[16] Journalist and author Phillip Knightley said Kosovo reporters were either "frothers or sheep," using the terms coined by British war correspondent Robert Fisk.

> Frothers had convinced themselves of the justice of NATO's war and the wickedness of President Milosovic and the Serbs. Their reporting was therefore both biased and predictable. The sheep stayed in Brussels, believed everything NATO told them, and defended NATO when anyone dared to suggest that NATO might be lying.[17]

The Rajmonda story is not unique. Earlier, for example, Penny Marshall of the British network ITN fabricated a story about Serbian concentration "death camps."[18]

The history, economics and politics surrounding these events are complicated, and cannot be adequately dealt with here. But perhaps we can provide a glimpse into the utter distortion, and refer readers to more details in the work of scholars such as Noam Chomsky, Michael Parenti and Edward Said.

To begin with recent events, it's revealing to examine the report, late in June, 2001, of the way in which the Yugoslavian cabinet handed over former president Slobodan Milosevic to the United Nations, for trial on war crimes charges. *The New York Times* reported that "The Yugoslav cabinet adopted a decree today committing itself to sending" Milosevic to the Hague. The cabinet decree came after the Yugoslavian parliament "failed to garner enough votes" [was democratically defeated] to pass a law allowing the extradition, and that both the parliamentary vote and cabinet decree were "precipitated by pressure from Western nations to demonstrate that the government was sincere in its cooperation with the tribunal before an international donor conference next week in Brussels."

The Times continued,

> The United States has indicated that it will not take part in the conference unless it is satisfied that the Yugoslav government has taken concrete action to cooperate with the tribunal. Without American participation, the Yugoslav government would have difficulty raising the $1 billion it needs to overhaul an economy that is in ruinous shape after 10 years of international sanctions, corrupt rule and regional conflicts...International pressure, namely the risk of losing United States economic assistance, pushed the authorities to arrest Mr. Milosevic on April 1. Since then, he has been in detention in Belgrade, under investigation for corruption and abuse of power.[19]

This despite the fact, as reported, that "...public opinion [in Yugoslavia] was firmly against sending Mr. Milosevic to the Hague. President Vojislav Kostunica was opposed to extraditing him and others to the tribunal, which he said was a political court and biased against Serbs."

So, to rephrase matters slightly, the U.S. used economic blackmail to force Yugoslavia, against the wishes of its people and its parliament, to extradite Milosevic for trial at the Hague. Of course, it is quite acceptable to be relatively open about these matters, because the former "dictator" is guilty of war crimes and has been disgraced. Any means, including blackmail, are warranted to bring him to "justice," even over the objections of his countrymen. The ends justify the means.

The London *Daily Telegraph* and Toronto *National Post* celebrated by claiming objectively, in a news story, that "For Mr. Milosevic's millions of victims, no punishment meted out by the United Nations court will be harsh enough."[20] For its part, *Maclean's* magazine demonstrated how completely it has adopted the NATO line.

In this brief account, Milosevic was demonized as the "butcher of the Balkans." Through reference to the Second World War, he was associated with Hitler's atrocities. Like other media accounts, this is selective, oversimplifying and distorting events. Reference is made to the "rule of law," ironically, by the very forces which chose to ignore the law when it was convenient. Each of these classic propaganda techniques was extensively promoted by the U.S. Administration and NATO, and in turn was reflexively embraced by the media.[22] The paragraph below is loaded with far-reaching assumptions and dubious suppositions that are beyond questioning. Surely, the use of the term "genocide" for what occurred in Croatia (as only one example) should warrant some circumspection, some regard for conditions that would justify such a description.

TYRANT IN THE DOCK

The man known as the "butcher of the Balkans" used raw violence to crush his opponents. But now, former Yugoslav President Slobodan Milosevic, 59, architect of the Balkan conflicts that produced Europe's most barbarous atrocities since the Second World War, will enter a courtroom and face the rule of law. Milosevic is the first former head of state to face trial at the UN War Crimes Tribunal in The Hague. He was turned over to tribunal representatives in Belgrade, flown to the Netherlands aboard a British plane and delivered by helicopter before dawn to a bleak, walled prison. The charges against Milosevic include crimes against humanity, in connection with the slaughter of civilians in Kosovo, and will likely be expanded to include genocide over atrocities committed in wars he waged against Bosnia and Croatia in the early 1990s.[21]

WHY BOMB?

But let us return to earlier events. To begin with, we will isolate the justifications for, and presentations of, the bombing itself. We were given to understand by the U.S. administration and the media of legitimation that the bombing was undertaken to stop the slaughter and displacement of the ethnic Albanians ("ethnic cleansing") by the Serbs, under Milosevic. As U.S. President Bill Clinton noted during the bombing, in a speech, "We cannot respond to such tragedies everywhere, but when ethnic conflict turns into ethnic cleansing where we can make a difference, we must try, and that is clearly the case in Kosovo."[23] *New York Times* global analyst Thomas Friedman wrote that "once the refugee evictions began, ignoring Kosovo would be wrong...and therefore using a huge air war for a limited objective was the only thing that made sense."[24] As Canada's foreign affairs minister, Lloyd Axworthy, put it: "We cannot stand by while an entire population is displaced, people are killed, villages are burned and looted, and a population is denied its basic rights because it does not belong to the 'right' ethnic group."[25]

The day after the bombing started, Olivia Ward of *The Toronto Star* indicated that NATO was merely making good on six months of "threats." Ward wrote, as her only sentence of explanation, in a descriptive account of the spectacle and destruction: "At least 20 targets in Serbia and Montenegro were hit by cruise missiles in the first hour, as six months of NATO threats to President Slobodan Milosevic to call off his offensive against ethnic separatists in Kosovo became a reality."[26]

The bombing was thus allegedly undertaken for humanitarian purposes, and only when peaceful negotiations had failed, in the form of the rejection of Rambouillet. This latter excuse is the "failed diplomacy" rationale which is familiar from the Gulf war and elsewhere.[27]

The standard media line is that "[FRY leader Slobodan] Milosevic's refusal to accept...or even discuss an international peacekeeping plan [namely, the Rambouillet Agreement] was what started [the] NATO bombing."[28] The bombing allegedly was undertaken because of rejection of the peace accord, and in order to prevent the ethnic cleansing. (An additional rationale was to re-establish the "credibility" of NATO, on the eve of its 50th anniversary, in April, 1999. More on this to follow.)

Haroon Siddiqui of the liberal *Toronto Star* immediately came down on the side of the war hawks the day after the bombing started, chastising NATO for its "dithering," and blaming Milosevic's intransigence, all the while applauding NATO's restraint:

By refusing to sign on [to Rambouillet] Milosevic has drawn the wrath of NATO's European and North American allies who have, finally, launched air strikes after months of dithering and issuing empty threats. Even after NATO's authorization to attack, one detected great reluctance among the allies to proceed, as though hoping for Milosevic to pull back at the last minute and avert the bombing.[29]

But the wording of the Rambouillet Agreement seems to have been designed to guarantee rejection. Its terms amounted to demands for an unconditional surrender by Milosevic, with complete military occupation and substantial political control of Kosovo by NATO, through its occupying force, KFOR. Here is just one example, taken from the text:

> The Parties invite the organization for Security and Cooperation in Europe (OSCE) through its Implementation Mission (IM) to monitor and supervise implementation of this Chapter and related provisions of this Agreement. The Chief of the Implementation Mission (CIM) or his designee shall have the authority to issue binding directives to the Parties and subsidiary bodies on police and civil public security matters to obtain compliance by the Parties with the terms of this Chapter. The Parties agree to cooperate fully with the IM and to comply with its directives.[30]

Robert Hayden, director of the Centre for Russian and East European Studies at the University of Pittsburgh, says a close reading of the Rambouillet accords shows that the text "provided for the independence of Kosovo in all but name and the military occupation by NATO of all of Yugoslavia—not just Kosovo." In his own detailed analysis of the text, Noam Chomsky agrees.[31]

Historian Barry Lituchy goes further. "I think the most obvious observation about [Rambouillet] is that it reveals a decades-long plan for reorganizing the Balkans region and for detaching Kosovo from Yugoslav sovereignty and governance."[32]

The Serbian National Assembly responded to the U.S./NATO ultimatum with a resolution rejecting the demand for NATO military occupation, and rejecting the West's demand for de facto partition, calling instead for a peaceful diplomatic settlement facilitated by the U.N. This counter offer went virtually unreported by the Western media.[33]

Afterwards, however, when the bombing had accomplished its task, the U.S. press finally acknowledged that the Rambouillet Agreement was "so fatally flawed that it helped precipitate what it was meant to prevent—the ethnic cleansing of Kosovo."[34]

So successful was the NATO/media campaign championing the "human rights" goal, that the five Canadian federal political parties arrived at a consensus favouring the bombing and Canadian armed forces involvement. It was not until early May, some five weeks into the bombing, that the avowed social democratic party, the New Democrats, finally broke ranks and called for an end to the bombing.[35]

The humanitarian motive is immediately suspect, because, contrary to *MediaThink*, it is totally out of character. As Chomsky and others have made abundantly clear, the historical record of the U.S. administration is one of greed, rape and pillage rather than resembling anything humanitarian. To quote one observer, Michael Parenti,

> [T]he U.S. national security state...has been involved throughout the world in subversion, sabotage, terrorism, torture, drug trafficking, and death squads...In the span of a few months, President Clinton bombed four countries: Sudan, Afghanistan, Iraq repeatedly, and Yugoslavia massively. At the same time, the U.S. was involved in proxy wars in Angola, Mexico (Chiapas), Colombia, East Timor, and various other places. And U.S. forces are deployed on every continent and ocean, with some 300 major overseas support bases—all in the name of peace, democracy, national security, and humanitarianism.[36]

This statement by Parenti contradicts the prevailing orthodoxy to the extent that it appears to be lunacy and borders on heresy, but it has been meticulously documented in painstaking detail by Parenti, Chomsky, myself and others.[37] William Blum has provided a brief but enlightening overview of international interventions by U.S. administrations, from 1945 to 1999. Blum notes that, "The engine of American foreign policy has been fuelled not by a devotion to any kind of morality, but rather by the necessity to serve other imperatives." Blum summarizes these goals, to which we shall return, as follows:

1) making the world safe for American corporations;

2) enhancing the financial statements of defense contractors at home who have contributed generously to members of congress;

3) preventing the rise of any society that might serve as a successful example of an alternative to the capitalist model;

4) extending political and economic hegemony over as wide an area as possible, as befits a "great power."[38]

Dr. Barry Lituchy has added a fifth goal, in the post-Soviet period: 5) the undermining and displacing of national sovereignty of countries around the world in favour of ever greater direct U.S. informal rule. As we will see, this is crucial to our discussion of the NATO attack on Kosovo.

Aside from the U.S. record and the apparent inconsistency, as numerous observers have pointed out: if the motives are humanitarian then why Kosovo, but not East Timor, or Chiapas, Chechnya, or Colombia? The humanitarian explanation really is untenable, especially in light of the (foreseeable) results of the bombing intervention, which only served to heighten the problems, the deaths and the displacement, which it was supposed to alleviate.

Another weakness in the humanitarian explanation is that the deaths and displacement really only began in earnest as a result of the bombing, rather than before it started. Hence, the causal sequence is reversed: the NATO bombing *resulted* in ethnic cleansing, rather than *responding* to it or alleviating it.

U.S.-NATO Commanding General Wesley Clark announced that it was "entirely predictable" that Serb terror and violence would intensify after the NATO bombing began. "The military authorities fully anticipated the vicious approach that Milosevic would adopt, as well as the terrible efficiency with which he would carry it out," Clark said.[39] According to Noam Chomsky, U.S. House of Representatives Intelligence Committee Chair Porter Gos told the media that:

> Our intelligence community warned us months and days before [the bombing] that we would have a virtual explosion of refugees over the 250,000 that was expected as of last year [pre-bombing], that the Serb resolve would increase, that the conflict would spread, and that there would be ethnic cleansing.[40]

A detailed retrospective in *The New York Times* concluded that, "The Serbs began attacking Kosovo Liberation Army strongholds on March 19, but their attack kicked into high gear on March 24, the night NATO began bombing Yugoslavia."[41] According to Edward Said, "No journalist has dared raise the question of how it is that the number of refugees has actually increased since the bombing began (the bombing that was supposed to save them), and any suggestion that NATO may have made matters worse is scarcely given a hearing."[42]

At *The Toronto Star*, Haroon Siddiqui chose to interview Bob Dole, former U.S. Republican candidate for the presidency, in a story which ran the day after the bombing started. Dole demonstrated that the repercussions of the bombing were well known:

> *Star*: What if Milosevic responds to the air bombing by attacking helpless Kosovars on the ground?
> *Dole*: I think that's a real possibility, knowing this mad man. I mean he can take it out on women and children and old people, as he did in Bosnia.[43]

Editorially, *The Star,* Canada's professedly "liberal" paper, justified Canadian involvement in the war. On the day of the bombing it intoned,

"Prime Minister Jean Chretien was right to make common cause with our allies to find a durable solution to this conflict. If that requires a prolonged NATO assault on Serb air defences, military installations and the heavy weapons that threaten civilians, so be it."[44] Within a few days, *The Star* provided a more elaborate defence of NATO's role in contravening its own charter, the illegal avoidance of the United Nations, alluding to the ethnic cleansing and more. The editorial is worth quoting at length.

> Slobodan Milosevic and his reckless, repressive government have presided over a decade of nationalist folly, destruction and death in the Balkans...That is why Canadian CF-18 fighter-bombers joined the first wave of North Atlantic Alliance air strikes last night against Milosevic's military forces, in NATO's first offensive action. The aim is to blunt Milosevic's ability to repeat Bosnia's carnage in Kosovo. Left unchecked, Milosevic's 30,000-strong forces in Kosovo—armed with tanks, rockets and artillery—will spread more terror and death in a region where 2,000 already have died...Split though the United Nations Security Council is on how to deal with Milosevic, the council has repeatedly demanded a ceasefire, an end to attacks on civilians, the withdrawal of troops and political negotiations for a peaceful settlement. Those demands grew tragically hollow as Milosevic's forces rampaged through burning villages, killing civilians. Ideally, the Security Council would have sanctioned NATO's strike. But Russia and China have always opposed military action. This encouraged Milosevic to renege on pledges he made to NATO last October to accept the Security Council's demands, and to resist NATO peacekeepers. Thus, from lack of resolve, a political dilemma degenerated into a human crisis. Canada and the rest of NATO have no reason to apologize for using force against those who would massacre civilians in Europe.[45]

"NATO's first offensive action," is the way *The Star* euphemistically applauded NATO's violation of its own charter, which authorizes the use of force in mutual self-defence only when one of its member states is attacked. NATO may resort to force either in self defense of a member state, or of a non-member state, so long as the government of that state requests NATO assistance.[46]

As for international law, well, *The Star* simply notes that, "Ideally, the Security Council would have sanctioned NATO's strike," seemingly oblivious to the fact that, without the UN's sanction, such force is illegal under international law. NATO cannot use force against another UN member state without that government's consent, if the action is not itself in defense of another UN member state, unless the action is specifically authorized by the UN Security Council.[47]

IGNORING 'LEGAL NICETIES'

Initially having more or less simply run with the NATO perspective, after the lapse of a day or two *The Toronto Star* felt compelled to justify NATO's (and its own position, taken in editorials and news columns), and to silence any niggling doubts over legal niceties. Hence, the paper ran a long Insight section article in which it addressed these concerns, and defended the war. *The Star* pointed out that "NATO, which was formed for the defence of Europe, for the first time took action against a sovereign country, in defence of human rights." The latter phrase is of course a qualifier which is meant to justify the former action. Who can be against "human rights?" Yes, admitted *The Star*, this is a war, "Launched by the North Atlantic Treaty Organization *democracies* against a small, stubborn, sovereign state that directly threatened no neighbour. And without the U.N. Security Council's authorization, in breach of the U.N. Charter."[48] The use of the usually redundant term "democracies" is intended to contrast with the FRY 'communists,' or 'dictatorship' without actually labelling them as such.

While acknowledging that "NATO clearly stands in technical breach of the U.N. Charter," (the intimation being that this is a mere technicality) *The Star* insisted "the council itself has lent legitimacy to NATO's action" by issuing three resolutions demanding that both sides cease hostilities, withdraw troops, and so forth. Just how it is that the U.N. could implicitly legitimize war by demanding hostilities cease, went unexplained.

The Star article asked whether we were seeing a new version of gunboat diplomacy? "Or does this mark something very different, and a lot healthier—the beginning of a more robust trend by the established democracies [there's that word again] to protect human rights everywhere?" Not wishing to obviously take sides, *The Star* appeared to sit on the fence. Its answer: "In the fog of war, it is impossible to say." But then of course, the article went on to take a very clear position legitimating NATO's actions: it appears to be a "robust trend."

This unofficial NATO defence required creative thinking. The letter of the law must not be confused with "its spirit," *The Star* writer argued. "Prime Minister Jean Chretien and the other 18 NATO leaders make a passionate, principled and unapologetic case that their decision to violate the letter of the U.N. Charter was necessary to honor its spirit." Apparently, this is about human rights and people's lives, and not about legal niceties. There is a growing global demand, *The Star* said, that "national sovereignty not remain a sacred altar upon which human security can be casually sacrificed." At least, not when it's someone else's national sovereignty.

Of course, just a few months later, national sovereignty was sacrosanct, even when it was non-existent: Indonesia and East Timor.

> [S]uddenly, the picture is exactly the opposite. From total disdain and contempt for sovereignty, in the case of Serbia—which by accident happens to be the only corner of Europe that's resisting U.S. plans for the region—we move to a client state, one of the major mass murderers of the modern period, and in this case concern for sovereignty is so exalted that we have to delicately observe it, even when there's no sovereignty at all.[49]

One must not get too bogged down by "the letter" of the law, especially when there are other considerations. "Canada and its close allies argue that while it certainly would have been preferable to get Security Council assent for the attack, respecting the letter of international law was one concern to be weighed among several. Another was NATO's credibility on this 50th anniversary of its founding," said *The Star*.

This disregard for international law is not novel, as Noam Chomsky has demonstrated. For example, John Kennedy advisor Dean Acheson justified the blockade of Cuba in 1962 by informing the American Society of International Law that the "propriety" of a U.S. response to a "challenge...[to the]...power, position, and prestige of the United States...is not a legal issue."[50] When the World Court was considering what it later condemned as Washington's "unlawful use of force" against Nicaragua in 1986, Secretary of State George Shultz ridiculed those who advocate "utopian, legalistic means like outside mediation, the United Nations, and the World Court, while ignoring the power element of the equation."[51]

The Star next launched into the (somewhat accurate) argument that impotence on the part of the U.N. was really nothing new, although it avoided explaining why this is so. "The U.N.'s impotence in Yugoslavia came as no news...the U.N. has often failed to keep the peace in the increasingly messy post-Cold War environment." Whether in the Balkans, Rwanda, Somalia or elsewhere, the problem seems to be "the Security Council's inability, or unwillingness, to intervene in timely fashion when crises develop," according to *The Star*. Noticeably absent from the newspaper's list of conflicts was Vietnam, or Iraq, Libya, Panama, Grenada, Nicaragua and various other examples of U.S. defiance of international law. Also missing was the plight of the Kurds at the hands of Turkey, which, unlike Kosovo, is within the bounds and jurisdiction of the NATO powers. No mention was made that the U.S. was perfectly happy with the United Nations as long as it was a docile instrument of U.S. power. As Senator William Fulbright commented in 1972, after he had become disaffected with U.S. policies, "Having controlled the United Nations for many years as tightly and as easily as a big-city boss controls his party machine, we had got used to the idea that the United Nations was a place where we could work our will."[52] In more recent years the U.S. has been subjected to the 'tyranny of the majority' (also known as democracy) at the U.N., despite its veto power, and has been increasingly isolated and embarrassed by its positions, if that is possible. Hence it has undermined the U.N. by withholding payment of dues and other measures. By comparison, NATO is a more elitist and malleable club to be cajoled or wielded as the case may be.

THE GRAY ZONE

The Star also saw matters as clearly defined, in what it described as "a classic Security Council split," with Yugoslavia and its friends on one side denouncing NATO's "illegal, brutal, unprovoked aggression." These allegations were left by *The Star* to stand, ghost-like, on their own, with no authoritative figures attached, although many could doubtless have been found at the nearest university. While on the other side, "NATO was unapologetic," *The Star* said, going on to quote Jeremy Greenstock, Britain's U.N. ambassador: "The action being taken is legal. It is justified as an exceptional measure to prevent an overwhelming humanitarian catastrophe." Then it turned to the Dutch ambassador, Peter van Walsum, who said NATO would "prefer to be able to base its action on a specific Security Council resolution. If, however, due to one or two permanent members' rigid interpretation of the concept of domestic jurisdiction, such a resolution is not attainable, we cannot sit back and simply let the humanitarian catastrophe occur." If only the Soviets and China would drop their "rigid interpretation" about national boundaries, and go along, then the U.S. could have its way with the U.N., transforming that body into the rapid strike force for which The Star yearns.

"So NATO's action, while in an uncomfortably gray zone, may not be nearly so recklessly unlawful as the Yugoslavs and their allies allege," *The Star* concluded. In closing, the article responded to criticism that NATO breached its own charter as a defensive alliance, and for having a double standard in not aiding oppressed separatist minorities farther afield in Kurdistan and East Timor. "All this is true enough," *The Star* allowed. "But since 1991, NATO has publicly asserted its intention to defuse 'crises inimical to European stability,' in addition to serving as a defensive shield for its members, while not being keen on venturing outside Europe's boundaries."[53]

It is important to recognize that "humanitarian motives" may have such distinct (if inaccurate) geographical boundaries.

All of the above could not have been more carefully or loyally crafted by the NATO Public Relations department itself. As in the case of East Timor, *The Toronto Star* was busily promoting "the consensus view."

According to Osgoode Law Professor Michael Mandel, "The first thing to note about NATO's war against Yugoslavia is that it was flatly illegal both in the fact that it was ever undertaken and in the way it was carried out. It was a gross and deliberate violation of international law and the Charter of the United Nations."[54]

The observant reader will wonder why, if the U.S. broke international law by bombing Kosovo, and civilians, it was not brought to justice? The U.S. and other NATO powers were brought before the World Court and charged with war crimes, but the case was rejected for technical reasons. The explanation was that the case was brought under the Genocide Convention, and the World Court requires that all parties to a dispute accept its jurisdiction, or otherwise it cannot adjudicate. The U.S. legal argument was that it doesn't accept the World Court jurisdiction, because even though it did sign the Genocide Convention, after a long delay, it signed with the condition that it was "inapplicable to the United States, unless agreed." And of course the agreement is never given. So the U.S. cannot be prosecuted in the World Court.[55]

A year after the fact, in June, 2000, *The Star* carried the following solitary sentence at the very end of a story about the condemnation of the bombings as criminal, by Amnesty International, and Human Rights Watch: "Yesterday, Britain's foreign affairs committee concluded the Kosovo war was morally just but illegal without U.N. authorization."[56]

THE CREDIBILITY FACTOR

Another rationale for the air war was that it was essential to NATO "credibility." This explanation was simply relayed by the media, usually without elaboration, question or challenge. For example, British PM Tony Blair told Parliament: "To walk away now would destroy NATO's credibility."[57] *The Toronto Star* said, "Having repeatedly warned Milosevic to stop attacking civilians, withdraw his troops, restore the self-government he yanked from Kosovo in 1989 and accept a peacekeeping force, NATO's credibility was firmly on the line when he continued to press his attack."[58] A *Globe and Mail* writer recited: "there was a genuine issue of NATO's credibility if it did not act against the new wave of ethnic cleansing in Kosovo."[59]

What the media and NATO implicitly mean by this is the ability of NATO to successfully threaten and entreat future 'dictators' such as Milosevic, to bring them into line and prevent their atrocities, without again being forced to resort to air wars. But there is another, more credible translation. Chomsky uses the apt if somewhat graphic analogy of a Mafia Don. Occasionally, you have to break a few legs.

> When a storekeeper does not pay protection money, the goons who are dispatched do not simply take the money: they leave him a broken wreck, so that others will get the message. Global Mafia Dons reason the same way, and understandably so. It is not, of course, that the Don needs the storekeeper's money. The common argument that this intervention must have been humanitarian because Kosovo has few significant resources or other use for the West reflects a serious misunderstanding of the basic elements of policy and recent history...One persistent concern is to establish "credibility," a requirement that becomes still more urgent if there is a perceived danger that the "rotten apple" might "spoil the barrel," that the "virus" of independence might "infect" others, in the terminology of high-level planners.[60]

One writer who misunderstands these basic elements is the ubiquitous Canadian internationalist Gwynne Dyer, who wrote a Focus section tribute to the war in April 1999 for *The Globe and Mail*. Dyer wrote that this war was not conducted "for oil or strategic advantage or any traditional goal of realpolitik, but simply to defend the lives and homes of two million Muslim peasants." For Dyer, the NATO propaganda and State Department spin is to be taken as gospel: no global Mafioso exists.

"There is certainly nothing of economic or strategic value in Kosovo," he wrote. But Dyer goes beyond this, to tout the new military humanism. As for legalities, Dyer is willing to look the other way during the current atrocities in the hope that the criminal acts of today will somehow miraculously be replaced by the rule of law tomorrow. "You can say this much for NATO: It is at least fighting an altruistic war, and one that may even have some bearing on whether the rule of law prevails internationally in the next century," Dyer wrote.[61] Across town on the pages of *The Toronto Star*, Dyer was arguing that the bombing of the Chinese Embassy was accidental, but that NATO was a bunch of cowards for bombing civilians from great heights, rather than putting troops on the ground and punishing Milosevic in a ground war.[62] A few months later, in September, Dyer wrote an apologetic for the Southam newspapers about how NATO's war in Kosovo was justified, but he said the situation in East Timor was different, and required the consent of the Indonesian government, whose military was slaughtering the East Timorese people.

> Do you remember what all the cynics said during the Kosovo war last spring? They said that NATO's attack on Serbia was not genuinely motivated by humanitarian concern about the slaughter of the Kosovars. They said it was really about oil, or strategy, or alliance solidarity, or any old thing that would allow them to deny that there was an element of altruism in American and Western foreign policy.[63]

Of course, Dyer had plenty of company. Writing in *Mother Jones* magazine in the U.S., long time leftist Todd Gitlin breathed a sigh of relief that "most of us" on the left, "supported the NATO war over Kosovo," because "we accepted the principle that the use of force was legitimate to protect human rights." Hence, the American left's "reflexive opposition to U.S. military intervention" dating back to Vietnam could now be dismissed as a rigid and unthinking "Absolute No" and "an excuse not to reason," by what he called "Rejectionists," such as Noam Chomsky and Howard Zinn, and "most of the contributors to *The Nation*."[64]

WAR CRIMES

There is very little space here for any detailed discussion or even overview of the numerous other problems with the prevailing orthodoxy on the war in Kosovo, but which in any case have been dealt with in books by Parenti, Chomsky, and others. A very brief list of these 'problems' would include: the labelling of the democratically-elected Milosevic as a "dictator;" the intervention in and distortion of his electoral defeat later; the hype over the Racak "massacre," which precipitated the war, but for which there turned out to be no evidence;[65] the Kosovo Liberation Army, (KLA) which went from "terrorists" to trusted allies overnight;[66] the similarity between the Rambouillet Accord, the Serbian National Assembly Resolution in response to it, and the final treaty, after all of the bombing; the way in which the U.S. ignored the final treaty; the May 7, 1999, intentional bombing of the Chinese Embassy in Belgrade, killing 3 civilians;[67] the deliberate bombing of the Belgrade headquarters of Radio Television Serbia on April 23, 1999, killing 16 civilian technicians, make-up artists, et cetera (NATO said the station was a military target because it broadcast propaganda); a NATO attack on a bridge at Varvarin on May 30, 1999, in which at least 11 civilians died: the bombing of a convoy of farm workers on the Djakovica-Prizen road where 75 died; the pounding of Korisa village, killing 87 refugees; the subsequent lack of evidence for the claimed "ethnic cleansing" and "genocide" supposedly perpetrated by Milosevic, *et cetera*.[68] The curious reader can find ample discussion and deconstruction of these events in the alternative media sources cited in this chapter.

Worth mention, however, before going on to briefly explain what the NATO war was really about, are the additional war crimes charges against NATO and its leaders, which were not pursued. The charges brought before the World Court and dismissed on a technicality are discussed above. Other charges against NATO were brought before the United Nations War Crimes Tribunal, which had indicted several weeks into the bombing and while the war was ongoing. Needless to say, the conduct of war itself must have made it extremely difficult if not impossible to investigate the grounds for laying charges, hence the hasty indictment was one of the factors undermining the credibility of the Tribunal from the outset. Additionally, as Christopher Black and Edward Herman point out, the "Tribunal's intervention declaring the Serb leadership to be guilty of war crimes was a public relations coup that justified the NATO policies and helped permit the bombing to continue and escalate." Concerning the indictment of NATO, Black and Herman noted that the investigation was focussed on the wrong area. "[T]he focus is on the conduct of NATO pilots and their commanders, not the NATO decision-makers who made the ultimate decisions to target the civilian infrastructure." The authors predicted in an article published five months in advance, what the decision would be. "We may rest assured that no indictments will result from this inquiry."[69]

Carla Del Ponte, Chief U.N. war crimes tribunal prosecutor announced to the Security Council in June 2000 that there would be no prosecutions against NATO. "Although some mistakes were made by NATO, I am very satisfied that there was no deliberate targeting of civilians or unlawful military targets by NATO during the bombing campaign," Del Ponte said. Amnesty International and a group of international lawyers led by Michael Mandel, a law professor at York University's Osgoode Law School, criticized the decision as a "setback" for international law and justice, and as unduly influenced by NATO.[70]

Of course, it's ridiculous to think that anyone who would be appointed to that office would have prosecuted NATO or the leaders of its member countries. That is not why she was appointed. As Diana Johnstone pointed out, "Indicting NATO would have meant biting the hand that feeds this Tribunal, whose former presiding judge Gabrielle Kirk McDonald once described Madeleine Albright as its 'mother.' It was hardly conceivable that the ICTY would allow itself to get too interested in crimes committed by the NATO powers who provide it with funding, equipment and investigators."[71]

Furthermore, it is not Del Ponte's world view. As Attorney-General of Switzerland for five years, *The Toronto Star* says Del Ponte "sent investigators after Saudi-born terrorism suspect Osama bin Laden for his alleged involvement in a deadly attack by Muslim militants on foreign tourists in the Egyptian resort of Luxor in 1997."[72] This one action shows she was on the side of the Clinton administration at the time. On Afghanistan's protection of bin Laden, the *Toronto Star* has this to say:

> At the instigation of Washington, the United Nations recently imposed crippling economic sanctions on the Taliban-led regime, including a ban on air traffic, further isolating the Afghan people from the world community. The U.N. action was linked to a U.S. ultimatum, insisting Kabul hand over Osama bin Laden, the Saudi militant allegedly responsible for the bombing of American embassies in Kenya and Tanzania in 1998.[73]

If Del Ponte would send her investigators after Osama bin Laden for Clinton, then why would she not do his bidding at the U.N.?

Even if Carla Del Ponte were not so inclined to support the Clinton administration, had she prosecuted NATO leaders, the U.S. administration would have vilified and ruined her personally, but more importantly they doubtless would have destroyed the U.N., in retribution. Knowing this to be true put Del Ponte and U.N. Secretary General Kofi Annan in a very precarious position.

Meanwhile, an independent tribunal in Berlin, presided over by a distinguished Hamburg University professor of international law, Dr. Norman Paech, was also deliberating. The Berlin Tribunal was supported by over sixty peace, civic and human rights groups. The panel of jurists, came from Austria, Italy, Hungary, Poland, Belarus, the Czech Republic, Russia and Macedonia.[74]

The verdict found the top officials of NATO and its member states guilty of violating all the relevant treaties and international agreements, from the United Nations Charter to the NATO Treaty itself, as well as numerous conventions. Far from being legitimately "humanitarian," NATO's intervention "ignored and blocked Belgrade's various compromise offers and dramatically worsened an already difficult situation, causing a sharp increase in the number of victims."[75]

As for civilian targets, the Berlin Tribunal cited statements from various NATO officials and military officers proving that the targeting of civilians was part of the "third stage" of a strategy to pressure the civilian population to rise up against its own government, "a clear violation of the Geneva Conventions." Weapons such as depleted uranium and cluster bombs also clearly endangered the civilian population, both during and after the actual bombing, and "constituted a particularly grave violation of international humanitarian law."[76]

A Canadian Newsdisc data base search of many Canadian newspapers, as well as the CBC and CTV television newscasts for all of 2000 and the first quarter of 2001, found no mention of the Berlin Tribunal or its chair, Dr. Norman Paech.

WHY THE WAR IN KOSOVO?

As the proffered explanations for the war in Kosovo have failed to withstand even minimal scrutiny, we are left with the question of what precipitated this apocalypse. To understand, we return to William Blum's four imperatives guiding the U.S. Administration's international interventions, listed above. Each of these is applicable in the current situation, but possibly none moreso than number 3) *preventing the rise of any society that might serve as a successful example of an alternative to the capitalist model.* To understand, we must discuss matters which "it wouldn't do to mention" in the corporate media, matters which are beyond the scope and ken of *MediaThink*.

The following lengthy quotation is taken, verbatim, and with permission, from the explanation offered by U.S. author Michael Parenti:

After World War II, socialist Yugoslavia became a viable nation and an economic success. Between 1960 and 1980 it had one of the most vigorous growth rates: a decent standard of living, free medical care and education, a guaranteed right to a job, one-month vacation with pay, a literacy rate of over 90 percent, and a life expectancy of 72 years. Yugoslavia also offered its multi-ethnic citizenry affordable public transportation, housing, and utilities, with a not-for-profit economy that was mostly publicly owned. This was not the kind of country global capitalism would normally tolerate. Still, socialistic Yugoslavia was allowed to exist for 45 years because it was seen as a nonaligned buffer to the Warsaw Pact nations.

The dismemberment and mutilation of Yugoslavia was part of a concerted policy initiated by the United States and the other Western powers in 1989. Yugoslavia was the one country in Eastern Europe that would not voluntarily overthrow what remained of its socialist system and install a free-market economic order. In fact, Yugoslavs were proud of their postwar economic development and of their independence from both the Warsaw Pact and NATO. The U.S. goal has been to transform the Yugoslav nation into a Third-World region, a cluster of weak right-wing principalities with the following characteristics:

• incapable of charting an independent course of self-development;

• a shattered economy and natural resources completely accessible to multinational corporate exploitation, including the enormous mineral wealth in Kosovo;

• an impoverished, but literate and skilled population forced to work at subsistence wages, constituting a cheap labour pool that will help depress wages in western Europe and elsewhere;

• dismantled petroleum, engineering, mining, fertilizer, and automobile industries, and various light industries, that offer no further competition with existing Western producers.

U.S. policymakers also want to abolish Yugoslavia's public sector services and social programs—for the same reason they want to abolish our public sector services and social programs. The ultimate goal is the privatization and Third Worldization of Yugoslavia, as it is the Third Worldization of the United States and every other nation. In some respects, the fury of the West's destruction of Yugoslavia is a backhanded tribute to that nation's success as an alternative form of development, and to the pull it exerted on neighbouring populations both East and West.

In the late 1960s and 1970s, Belgrade's leaders, not unlike the Communist leadership in Poland, sought simultaneously to expand the country's industrial base and increase consumer goods, a feat they intended to accomplish by borrowing heavily from the West. But with an enormous IMF debt came the inevitable demand for "restructuring," a harsh austerity program that brought wage freezes, cutbacks in public spending, increased unemployment, and the abolition of worker-managed enter- prises. Still, much of the economy remained in the not-for-profit public sector, including the Trepca mining complex in Kosovo, described in the New York Times as "war's glittering prize...the most valuable piece of real estate in the Balkans...worth at least $5 billion" in rich deposits of coal, lead, zinc, cadmium, gold, and silver.[77]

That U.S. leaders have consciously sought to dismember Yugoslavia is not a matter of speculation but of public record. In November 1990, the Bush administration pressured Congress into passing the 1991 Foreign Operations Appropriations Act, which provided that any part of Yugoslavia failing to declare independence within six months would lose U.S. financial support. The law demanded separate elections in each of the six Yugoslav republics, and mandated U.S. State Department approval of both election procedures and results as a condition for any future aid. Aid would go only to the separate republics, not to the Yugoslav government, and only to those forces whom Washington defined as "democratic," meaning right-wing, free-market, separatist parties.[78]

It is easy to see how the above explanation offered by Michael Parenti supports William Blum's general observations on U.S. policy. Parenti's views provide an especially good fit with Blum's third imperative, although they are also consistent—as is Chomsky's explanation of the role of "NATO credibility"—with the other three. Other authors are in general agreement as well, including Michel Chossudovsky, professor of political economy at the University of Ottawa, Barry Lituchy, a historian who teaches at the City University of New York, and others.[79]

There is also a telling contrast between this account and, coincidentally, that of the corporate, free-market press. Recall too, for example, the explanation by the CBC's Carol Off, which was simply that, "As Yugoslavia disintegrated in the 1990s, each region declared independence." Things just happen. Or, they happen because of the actions of brutal dictators such as Milosevic, and the response by freedom fighters such as Rajmonda. Carol Off, Nancy Durham and all of the mainstream media are seemingly unaware of the broader machinations of economic power documented by Parenti, Lituchy, Chomsky, Chossudovsky, and others, although these viewpoints are no further away than their fingertips.[80]

The conclusions drawn about the NATO bombing by Osgoode law professor Michael Mandel are also consistent with Blum's formulations, and those of Chomsky, Parenti, Herman and others. In his testimony before the Standing Committee on Foreign Affairs of the Canadian House of Commons, Mandel noted:

The most plausible explanation then is that this attack was not about the Balkans at all. It was an attempt to overthrow the authority of the

United Nations and make NATO, and therefore the United States, the world's supreme authority, to establish the "precedent" that NATO politicians have been talking about since the bombing stopped. To give the United States the free hand that the United Nations does not, in its conflicts with the Third World and its rivalries with Russia, China and even Europe. In other words, this was not a case of the United Nations being an obstacle to humanitarianism. It was a case of using a flimsy pretext of humanitarianism to overthrow the United Nations.[81]

It is easy to see how undermining the U.N. served all five of the above imperatives, from improving conditions for U.S. corporations generally, to funding defence contractors, preventing alternatives to capitalism, extending U.S. political-economic hegemony, and supplanting nationalism in favour of globalization.[82]

I should indicate that there is no single, predominant analysis by the left of the complex events surrounding the bombing of Kosovo. Although I have noted that there is considerable agreement on some matters, particularly in opposition to the simplistic portrayal by the corporate media, the independent thinkers in academia whom I have cited here are not all in uniform agreement. For example, in part, Michael Parenti feels that Noam Chomsky is too critical of Slobodan Milosevic because he says Chomsky uncritically absorbed some aspects of the corporate media portrayal.

In addition to the five imperatives above, there are also specific considerations, such as justifying Albanian terrorism, as mentioned above, or the drive for a Greater Albania. Barry Lituchy elaborated in commenting on a draft version of this chapter in August, 2001.

Is this the first time that U.S.- backed terrorists have used the U.S. media to lie about their cause? Is it the most successful example? These are interesting questions because the Albanian terrorist movement is far from finished—it is at war today in Macedonia and has its sights on Montenegro and Greece tomorrow. Let me just throw a question in here...The one issue that the U.S. media not only do not report on, but painstakingly cover up at every turn, is the drive for a Greater Albania. Why is the Western media so determined to suppress this information? The answer is clear: its forces are not only the fascist vanguard and U.S.- backed agency that is driving the violence in the Balkans, it is also the immediate foreign policy objective of the NATO establishment.[83]

The drive for a Greater Albania is indeed absent from corporate media accounts.

One of the sad things is that there is little in the least that is novel about any of this, with the possible exception of the increased level of barbarity, and, despite claims to the contrary, the improved technological precision of the bombing, which destroyed public buildings but left private ones intact. Otherwise, we have seen it all before, during the Gulf War, in Vietnam, Panama, and elsewhere. New "monsters" are created, whether it is Saddam Hussein, Manuel Noriega, Daniel Ortega, or Slobodan Milosevic. Under the pretext of "humanitarian purposes," whether that means saving the domestic population from communism (Vietnam), saving an invaded country from one dictator only to restore another (Kuwait), or simply bringing to justice a former best friend and trading partner-turned -drug-thief (Panama),[84] civilian populations are bombed, the "virus" or rotten apple is contained, and others are taught a valuable lesson.

Almost a decade ago, I wrote an analysis of media coverage of the Gulf War, in which there were many similar observations: the names and the places have changed, but the methods are strikingly similar. Saddam Hussein was once, like Milosevic, a favoured friend and trading partner, but when circumstances changed, he had to be demonized, just as the "Huns" had to be demonized during the World Wars. These are the "stark terms of good and evil" in war reporting, to quote British journalist Phillip Knightley, who goes on to conclude, "in wars in which a war correspondent's own country is involved, the sensible thing for the reader or viewer to do is to regard those correspondents as government propagandists and believe little or nothing of what they report."[85] In the Gulf, civilian targets were bombed, and we were told that it was Hussein's fault for duping people into hiding out in military targets, an argument which can be traced back to the Vietnam "conflict" as well.[86] Just as Britain bombed German civilians in World War II, and denied it.

When electrical transformers in Belgrade were intentionally bombed, a U.S. spokesperson said it was to force the Serbs "to put pressure on their leadership to end this," just as Iraq was pulverized and held hostage by a boycott in an attempt to force its people to put pressure on Saddam Hussein, punishing the people for their leadership.[87] What punishment will be dealt to the American people, in return for being saddled with Bush II? Or to Canadians, for repeatedly electing Jean Chretien?

With the Gulf war, ("Operation Desert Storm,") we had "Nayirah," 15, who turned out to be the daughter of the Kuwaiti ambassador to the U.S., who (with the help of the PR firm Hill and Knowlton) duped the U.S. Congressional Human Rights Caucus and the American people into believing an invented story about the barbarism of the Iraqis. In Kosovo, we had Rajmonda, 18. In the Gulf as in the FRY, bombing was portrayed as a "final resort," after the "extraordinary" diplomatic efforts had been tried and failed, due to the unreasonableness of the madmen on the other side. In reality, the negotiations were a sham, a demand for total capitulation and subjugation which was designed to fail, and to leave no apparent alternative but the bomb. Hussein 'had' to be bombed to prevent him from taking over another country and murdering infants. Milosevic 'had' to be bombed to prevent him from the genocide of ethnic Albanians. During both wars, anti-war protests were all but ignored by the media. "One hundred thousand people in the streets of Rome including 182 members of the Italian parliament," wrote John Pilger in *The Guardian*. "Thousands in Greece and Germany, protests taking place every night in colleges and town halls across Britain. Almost none of it is reported."[88]

In short, the U.S. Administration and its collaborators in other governments and the media conducted yet another massive and successful propaganda campaign to justify their international terror. As indicated, there is little new about their methods,[89] and the media have kept to their traditional, supportive—nay, servile—role. British journalist Phillip Knightley says there is a crisis.

> The lies, manipulation, news management, propaganda, spin, distortion, omission, slant and gullibility of the coverage of this war, so soon after the media debacle in the Gulf, has brought the media and war correspondents to a crisis point in their history.[90]

Of course, it's not just a journalistic crisis, but a crisis in accountability, public discourse, nationalism, (in the sense of community) democracy, anti-globalization, social justice, life and death. As Dr. Diana Johnstone has indicated, the success of the "humanitarian intervention" lie, that essential aspect of the propaganda, may be gauged by looking at the contrast between anti-WTO protests in Seattle and anti-NATO protests, in 1999. The protests in Seattle against the World Trade Organization (and subsequent demonstrations in Windsor, Ontario, Quebec City and Genoa) confirmed that a massive popular movement has developed opposing "globalization." But the people who took to the streets in Seattle in December, 1999, by and large, were not out on the streets protesting the NATO war in Yugoslavia the previous spring. This despite the fact that Kosovo was an integral part of the forced globalization which they oppose.[91] It is relatively easy to observe the effects of free trade, as we have had more than a decade of experience with it in North America, where it has brought falling income (for workers), lost jobs, increased insecurity and inequality. Here, we have real world experience to contrast with the glowing accounts in the corporate media. Not so with the relatively recent, more complex, fleeting and heavily propagandized international "humanitarian" efforts. But, according to Johnstone, "This makes our task clear: we need to make our people understand that NATO is the military arm of an unjust, undemocratic and destructive economic globalization."

Kept unaware by the media of these contemporary facts and this history, we are powerless to prevent their repetition and to change things for the better.

NOTES

1. Nancy Durham's stories on Rajmonda, complete with text, pictures and some real audio, may be found at http://tv.cbc.ca/national/pgminfo/kosovo3/rajmonda.html

2. Nancy Durham, *The truth about Rajmonda*, Brian Stewart, anchor, *The National Magazine*, CBC-TV, September 8, 1999.

3. Paul Waldie, "CBC Airs Documentary to Explain Error in Stories from Kosovo: Teen's False Claims Discovered During Follow-up Story," *The National Post*, September 9, 1999."

4. I am grateful to historian Barry Lituchy for this observation about the documentary, in personal correspondence, August, 2001.

5. Nancy Durham, *The truth about Rajmonda*.

6. Quoted in, Michael Chossudovsky, "Kosovo 'Freedom Fighters' Financed By Organized Crime,"April 8, 1999. http://www.ius.bg.ac.yu/apel/materijali/kla.html#drugs

7. http://cbc.ca/onair/personalities/national/durham.html

8. Brian Stewart, "Foreign Snapshots," *The National Magazine*, CBC-TV, December 28, 1999. Emphasis added.

9. Chris Hedges, "Inside the Kosovo Liberation Army: Kosovo's Next Masters," *Foreign Affairs, 78:3,* May/June 1999.
http://www.nettime.org/nettime.w3archive/199905/msg00154.html

10. Quoted in Phillip Knightley, "The media—NATO's willing accomplice?" Speech at the Committee for Peace in the Balkans," Public Seminar, House of Commons, London, June 27, 2000. Knightley is the author of *The First Casualty: the War Correspondent as Hero and Mythmaker from Crimea to Kosovo*, Prion Books, London, 2000. http://www.geocities.com/cpa_blacktown/20000709zzzpkcpbuk.htm.

11. Noam Chomsky, *The New Miliary Humanism: Lessons From Kosovo*, Common Courage Press, Monroe, ME, 1999, p. 31.

12. Peter Mansbridge, "Kosovo's historical importance," *The National*, CBC-TV, March 24, 1999, with Carol Off reporting.

13. American author Michael Parenti toured the FRY in August, 1999, and provided a personal account of the damage. See Michael Parenti, "Yugoslav Sojourn: Notes from the Other Side," January 2000,
http://www.michaelparenti.org/YugoslavSojourn.html. See also, Michael Parenti, *To Kill a Nation: The Attack on Yugoslavia*, Verso, N.Y., 2001.

14. Gregory Elich and Barry Lituchy (Eds) *Interviews and Testimonies: An Investigation of US and NATO War Crimes in Yugoslavia*, 2000, pp. 75-77.

15. Anthony Goodman, "No war crimes probe into NATO bombing: U.N. tribunal defends actions in Yugoslavia," *The Toronto Star*, June 3, 2000.

16. Edward Said, "The blind misleading the blind," *The New Statesman*, May 17th, 1999.

17. Phillip Knightley, "The media..."

18. For an expose on the Serb concentration death camps, see www.emperors-clothes.com/news/film.htm

19. Carlotta Gall, "Yugoslavs Act on Hague Trial for Milosevic," *The New York Times*, June 24, 2001.

20. Julius Strauss, "A family of ruthless cunning: Wife closest ally: A quarter of a million citizens were murdered," *The National Post*, June 29, 2001.

21. "Tyrant in the Dock," *Maclean's*, July 9, 2001. For another perspective see Stan Goff, "Who is Guilty? Milosovic? Or NATO?" http://emperors-clothes.com/articles/goff/goff.htm

22. For an overview of propaganda techniques, and their application to the U.S. media and Bosnia, see Carl Kosta Savich, "War, Journalism and Propaganda: An Analysis of Media Coverage of the Bosnian and Kosovo Conflicts," June, 2000. http://www.freerepublic.com/forum/a39adeffd2670.htm

23. Clinton in *The New York Times*, May 23, 1999. Quoted in Chomsky, *Military Humanism*, p. 3.

24. Thomas Friedman, "Foreign Affairs," *The New York Times*, June 4, 1999. Quoted by Noam Chomsky, *The New Miliary Humanism: Lessons From Kosovo*, Common Courage Press, Monroe ME, 1999, p.5.

25. Gordon Barthos "The worst nightmare," *The Toronto Star*, March 27, 1999.

26. Olivia Ward, "Air of confusion sweeps Belgrade streets," *The Toronto Star*, March 25, 1999.

27. Cf. James Winter, "Truth as the First Casualty," in *Common Cents: Media Portrayal of the Gulf War and Other Events*, Black Rose Books, Montreal, 1992.

28. Craig Whitney, writing in *The New York Times,* quoted by Noam Chomsky, "Kosovo Peace Accord," *Z Magazine*, July 99.

29. Haroon Siddiqui, "Blunt talk about Kosovo from Bob Dole," *The Toronto Star*, March 25, 1999.

30. Taken from The Rambouillet Accord, "Interim Agreement for Peace on Self-government in Kosovo," Rambouillet, France, February 23, 1999, http://www.swans.com/library/art6/rambouil.html. For a discussion of the accord, see Noam Chomsky, *The New Miliary Humanism: Lessons From Kosovo*, Common Courage Press, Monroe ME, 1999, p. 106+.

31. Robert Hayden, "Did Allies Demand Right to Occupy All of Yugoslavia?" The Institute for Public Accuracy, Washington DC, April 27, 1999. http://www.diaspora-net.org/food4thought/expert_opinion.htm

See also, Chomsky, *Military Humanism*, pp. 106+.

32. Barry Lituchy, personal correspondence, August, 2001.

33. Chomsky, *Military Humanism*, pp. 108-9. Chomsky notes, "Several database searches have found scarce mention, none in the national press and major journals."

34. Editorial, *The Boston Globe*, June 18, 1999. Quoted by Chomsky, *Military Humanism*, p. 108.

35. Allan Thompson and Edison Stewart, "Suspend strikes on Yugoslavia, NDP says: McDonough breaks consensus in Parliament," *The Toronto Star,* May 4, 1999.

36. Michael Parenti, "The Rational Destruction of Yugoslavia," November, 1999 http://www.michaelparenti.org/yugoslavia.html

37. See the Parenti and Chomsky works cited in this chapter. Also, James Winter, *Common Cents: Media Portrayal of The Gulf War and Other Events*, Black Rose Books Montreal, 1992.

38. William Blum, "A Brief History of United States Interventions, 1945 to the Present, *Z-Magazine*, June, 1999. http://www.zmag org/

39. Chomsky, *Military Humanism*, pp. 20-21. Chomsky quotes Clark from *The New York Times*, March 27, 1999.

40. Quoted in Chomsky, *Military Humanism*, p. 22.

41. Ibid.

42. Said, "The blind misleading the blind."

43. Siddiqui, "Blunt Talk."

44. Editorial, "Serb assault on Kosovo puts NATO to shame," *The Toronto Star*, March 23, 1999.

45. Editorial, "Milosevic's folly," *The Toronto Star*, March 25, 1999.

46. Taken from the complaint filed before the Prosecutor of the International Criminal Tribunal for the Former Yugoslavia, charging NATO's political and military leaders and all responsible NATO personnel with grave breaches of the Geneva Convention of 1949 and violations of the laws and customs of war, Athens, May 3, 1999. www.znet.org/

47. Complaint, International Criminal Tribunal.

48. Gordon Barthos "The worst nightmare..." *The Toronto Star,* March 27, 1999. Emphasis added.

49. Noam Chomsky, "Sovereignty and World Order," a speech delivered at Kansas State University, Manhattan, Kansas September 20, 1999. www.znet.org

50. Chomsky, *The New Military Humanism*, p. 151.

51. Ibid, p. 153.

52. Quoted in Noam Chomsky, *Necessary Illusions*, Appendix 4, CBC, Toronto, 1989. http://www.zmag.org/chomsky/ni/ni-c09-s09.html

53. Gordon Barthos "The worst nightmare..."

54. Michael Mandel, Testimony before the Standing Committee on Foreign Affairs and International Trade, House of Commons, Canada, February 22, 2000. http://www.balkanpeace.org/content/otkh02.shtml

55. Chomsky, "Sovereignty and World Order."

56. Steven Erlanger, "NATO bomb raids that killed civilians labelled 'deliberate': International law broken: Amnesty report," *The Toronto Star*, July, 2000.

57. Blaine Harden, "Crisis in The Balkans: Doing The Deal—A special report.; A Long Struggle That Led Serb Leader to Back Down," *The New York Times*, June 6, 1999. Quoted in Chomsky, *The New Military Humanism*, p.134.

58. Gordon Barthos "The worst nightmare..."

59. Gwynne Dyer, At Last: A Good War, *The Globe and Mail*, April 17, 1999.

60. Chomsky, *The New Military Humanism*, pp. 135-36.

61. Gwynne Dyer, "At last: A Good War."

62. Gwynne Dyer, "NATO strategy is coward's way to wage war," *The Toronto Star*, May 13, 1999.

63. Gwynne Dyer, "West can't go into East Timor the way NATO did in Kosovo," Victoria *Times Colonist*, September 11, 1999.

64. Todd Gitlin, "The end of the absolute no," *Mother Jones*, October, 1999.

65. For an excellent discussion of Racak and other distortions, see Parenti, *To Kill a Nation*.

66. Robert Gelbard, the Clinton Administration's former special envoy for Kosovo, told Agence France Presse in February 1998 that the KLA "is, without any questions, a terrorist group." Quoted in, Michael Chossudovsky, "Kosovo 'Freedom Fighters' Financed By Organized Crime,"April 8, 1999. http://www.ius.bg.ac.yu/apel/materijali/kla.html#drugs

67. "Truth behind America's raid on Belgrade," *Guardian Unlimited,* November 28, 1999, http://www.guardian.co.uk/Archive/Article/0,4273,3935955,00.html. Richard Gwyn of *The Toronto Star* reacted with horror when NATO bombed the Chinese Embassy in Belgrade, killing three civilians. But he was horrified at the Chinese government for allegedly using the incident for propaganda purposes. "This kind of governmental opportunism isn't in the least novel," Gwyn noted. He went on to declare with finality that despite the politics, "Nevertheless, the attack on the Chinese embassy in Belgrade and the killing of three journalists there, was an accident." Richard Gwyn, "China Reveals Much in Reaction to Bombing," *The Toronto Star*, May 14, 1999. For a discussion about how Gwyn handled the lack of evidence for Serb atrocities see Jared Israel, "The Obligatory Bash: Etiquette for a Brave New World," November 8, 1999. http://emperors-clothes.com/analysis/obligato.htm

68. See, for example, John Laughland, "The Massacres That Never Were," *The Spectator*, London, October 25, 1999.

http://www.bhhrg.org/press-articles/press1999/massacres_that_never_were.htm

69. Christopher Black and Edward Herman, "An Unindicted War Criminal: Louise Arbour and the International Crimes Tribunal," *Z Magazine*, February 2000. http://www.zmag.org/ZMag/articles/feb2000herman.htm

70. Anthony Goodman, "No war crimes probe into NATO bombing: U.N. tribunal defends actions in Yugoslavia," *The Toronto Star*, June 3, 2000.

71. Diana Johnstone, "The Berlin Tribunal: More Serious than the Hague," Z-Net, June 30, 2000 http://www.zmag.org/ZSustainers/ZDaily/2000-06/30Johnstone.htm

72. Quoted in, Janet McBride, "Arbour tenacious as human rights warrior: Arrest of suspect caps last days as chief prosecutor," *The Toronto Star*, September 3, 1999.

73. Harry Sterling, "U.S. policies come with high price tag," *The Toronto Star*, November 26, 1999.

74. Johnstone, "The Berlin Tribunal."

75. Quotes are taken from Johnstone, "The Berlin Tribunal."

76. *Ibid.*

77. *The New York Times*, July 8, 1998, quoted in Parenti, "The Rational Destruction of Yugoslavia."

78. I have quoted Michael Parenti at length, and verbatim here from his article, "The Rational Destruction of Yugoslavia," November, 1999. For an elaboration, see also, Michael Parenti, *To Kill a Nation: The Attack on Yugoslavia*, Verso, N.Y., 2001. Http://www.michaelparenti.org/yugoslavia.html. (Used with the permission of Verso Publishers.)

79. Cf. Michel Chossudovsky, "Nato Has Installed a Reign of Terror in Kosovo," *Voices Against the War in Kosovo*, 08/10/99, www.softmakers.com/fry/docs/chossudovsky.htm, which also contains numerous links to other articles. Michel Chossudovsky and Barry Lituchy were both interviewed during the war on the radio program, *Making Contact*. You may access the audio program or transcript at: National Radio Project, *Making Contact* Transcripts, April 13, 1999, #15-99: "Morality or Western Interests: NATO in Yugoslavia," http://www.radioproject.org/transcripts/9915.html.

    See also, Michel Chossudovsky, *The Globalization of Poverty*, Common Courage Press, N.Y., 2001.

80. I'm aware that I have lumped in the CBC, which is partially publicly funded, with the corporate, "pro-free enterprise" press. As I have elaborated elsewhere, for a variety of reasons the differences are small and diminishing. See James Winter, *Democracy's Oxygen: How Corporations Control The News*, Black Rose Books, Montreal, 1997.

81. Michael Mandel, "Testimony before the Standing Committee on Foreign Affairs."

82. For an elaboration on this topic, see Chapter 16 in Parenti, *To Kill A Nation*.

83. Barry Lituchy, personal correspondence, August, 2001. Lituchy made similar comments on Dennis Bernstein's KPFA radio program *Flashpoints,* in June 2001.

84. For example, in justifying the 1989 U.S. invasion of Panama, ABC TV's Ted Koppel opined that "Manuel Noriega belongs to that special fraternity of international villains, men like Qaddafi, Idi Amin, and the Ayatollah Khomeini, whom Americans just love to hate." So, Koppel concluded, "strong public support for a reprisal [sic] was all but guaranteed." Colleague Peter Jennings denounced Noriega as "one of the more odious creatures with whom the United States has had a relationship," while CBS's Dan Rather placed him "at the top of the list of the world's drug thieves and scums." Cited in Noam Chomsky, *Deterring Democracy*, Verso, N.Y., 1991, pp. 145, 151.

85. Phillip Knightley, "The media—NATO's willing accomplice?" Speech at the Committee for Peace in the Balkans," Public Seminar, House of Commons, London, June 27, 2000. Knightley is the author of *The First Casualty: the War Correspondent as Hero and Mythmaker from Crimea to Kosovo*, Prion Books, London, 2000. http://www.geocities.com/cpa_blacktown/20000709zzzpkcpbuk.htm

86. Cf. "Truth as the First Casualty," in James Winter, *Common Cents: Media Portrayal of the Gulf War and Other Events*, Black Rose Books, Montreal, 1992.

87. Quoted in Phillip Knightley, "The media…" Knightley quotes U.S. spokesperson Kenneth Bacon.

88. *Ibid.*

89. For an overview of propaganda techniques, and their application to the U.S. media and Bosnia, in an historical context, see in Carl Kosta Savich, "War, Journalism and Propaganda:An Analysis of Media Coverage of the Bosnian and Kosovo Conflicts," http://www.serbianna.com/savich/stories/war_journalism.html, June 2000.

90. Phillip Knightley, "The media…"

91. Diana Johnstone, "The Mixed Motives behind NATO's War against Yugoslavia," *The Review of International Affairs*, April-June, 2000.
http://www.geocities.com/cpa_blacktown/20000716djohnriayu.htm

CHAPTER FOUR

NELLIE McCLUNG ROLLS OVER

"[A] trite example but a helpful example, is the idea of borrowing a car. If I want to borrow your car...I assume you are not consenting to me borrowing your car until you say yes. I don't assume that you are consenting to me using your car until you say no. And we think the implication of this decision, the lower court's decision, is that there is this presumption that women are walking around in a constant state of consent to sexual activity, until they can convince somebody that they are not consenting."[1]

Barbara McDonald, 17, was walking through the parking lot of the Heritage Mall in Edmonton, where she had been shopping with her room-mate, when they were hailed by a middle aged man. Steve Ewanchuk, 44, approached the two young women and asked them if they would like a job selling furniture at his shop in the mall. Her roommate said she was interested, and exchanged phone numbers with Ewanchuk. The next day, Ewanchuk called their home and as her roommate was sleeping, Barbara agreed to go to a job interview back at the mall. She suggested they talk in the mall, but Ewanchuk, the prospective employer, urged her to meet with him in his van in the parking lot where they would have more privacy. Reluctantly, Barbara agreed to talk in the van, but left the door open as she

107

felt uncomfortable. She told Ewanchuk that she was the mother of a six-month-old baby and that, along with her boyfriend, she shared an apartment with her roommate.

It was a hot day in June, 1994, and Barbara was wearing shorts and a T-shirt. Ewanchuk urged her to continue the interview in his trailer, which was hitched to the van, so that he could show her a catalogue and some of the items she would be selling. Again reluctantly, Barbara agreed. When they entered the trailer, Barbara left the door open but Ewanchuk appeared to lock it behind her, and she began to get alarmed. She had recently watched a TV program on the Discovery Channel, which advised women not to show their fear in such situations. So, not wanting to appear afraid or to anger Ewanchuk, who was twice her size, she agreed to massage his shoulders. He said he would reciprocate, and started to massage her, bringing his hands close to her breasts. At this point, Barbara pushed him away with her elbows and said "no."

Ewanchuk told Barbara to lie down, and began massaging her feet. Again out of fear, she complied. The touching progressed to her inner thigh and pelvic area up to a point where he laid heavily on top of her and started grinding his pelvic area against hers while telling her, "I could get you so horny so that you would want it so bad, and I wouldn't give it to you because I have self-control and because I wouldn't want to give it to you."

"Just please stop," Barbara told him.

"I had you worried, didn't I? You were scared, weren't you?" he said.

"Yes, I was very scared," she agreed. Ewanchuk told Barbara not to be afraid, and asked her if she trusted that he wouldn't hurt her. She said, "Yes, I trust that you won't hurt me."

At this point, Ewanchuk hugged her, and then suddenly resumed his pelvic grinding, only this time he tried to touch her vaginal area. He pulled out his penis and pushed it up under her shorts, rubbing against her underwear.

"No! Stop!" Barbara said. And finally, he did. He stood up, smiled at her and said, "It's okay. See, I'm a nice guy, I stopped." He again hugged

Barbara lightly before opening up his wallet and removing a $100 bill, which he gave to her. He said the $100 was for the massage, and told her not to tell anyone about it. He made some reference to another female employee with whom he also had a very close and friendly relationship, and said he hoped to get together with Barbara again. She asked him to open the door and he did. After a few minutes more of awkward conversation outside the trailer, she left, and hurried home, crying. She told her roommate what happened. Then the phone rang. It was Ewanchuk. He wanted to know if she was okay. She said she was fine. Then she hung up and called the police.[2]

CONSTANT CONSENT

Ewanchuk was charged with sexual assault. Aside from the uncontested events in the above account of what happened, two things pointed towards a conviction. First, there was Ewanchuk's record. He had three rape convictions and one previous conviction for sexual assault, in 1989. After his third rape conviction in 1973, he served a ten-year prison sentence. In addition, there were five assault complaints against Ewanchuk on record in the 1980s and 1990s, which were investigated but led to no charges.[3] Second, there was new federal legislation in place, enacted in 1992, which was termed the "No-means-No" Bill. The new law placed the onus on the initiator of sex to reasonably secure consent.

But the trial judge, Justice John Moore of Alberta Court of Queen's Bench, acquitted Ewanchuk, in part because Barbara McDonald's dress and behaviour had "implied consent." Ewanchuk's lawyer advised him against testifying, which prevented his past convictions from being introduced. The prosecution appealed but Ewanchuk's acquittal was upheld in a split decision (2-1) by the Alberta Court of Appeal, in 1998.

In a dissenting opinion, Chief Justice Catherine Fraser said women don't walk the streets of Canada in a state of constant consent. Nor can an initial rejection be seen to be an invitation to an increased level of sexual activity or else it would signal a return to the rejected myth that "no really means try harder."

But in his opinion, Judge John McClung indicated that Barbara Mc-Donald (not her real name) brought the assault on herself, by virtue of her appearance. "It must be pointed out that the complainant did not present herself to Ewanchuk or enter his trailer in a bonnet and crinolines," wrote McClung. (Crinolines were a petticoat-type undergarment common in the Victorian era). He said Ewanchuk could not be expected to read Barbara's mind. "There is no room to suggest that Ewanchuk knew, yet disregarded, her underlying state of mind as he furthered *his romantic intentions*." McClung, who is the grandson of the famous Alberta suffragist Nellie McClung, referred to Ewanchuk's assault as "clumsy passes," and said that although his actions "would hardly raise Ewanchuk's stature in the pantheon of chivalric behaviour," he concluded that "the sum of the evidence indicates that Ewanchuk's advances to the complainant were far less criminal than hormonal." McClung said that "every advance he made to her stopped when she spoke against it" and that "[t]here was no evidence of an assault or even its threat." And he said the matter was best dealt with by the young woman herself: she should have used physical force. "In a less litigious age going too far in the boyfriend's car was better dealt with on site—a well-chosen expletive, a slap in the face or, if necessary, a well-directed knee."

Judge McClung also was at the centre of another controversial ruling, his 1996 ruling on Delwin Vriend, a gay man fired from his college teaching job. McClung rejected a lower Alberta court's redrafting of Alberta's human rights act, to include gay rights. Judge McClung denounced "constitutionally hyperactive judges pronouncing [on] all our emerging laws according to their own values" and railed against "crusading...ideologically determined judges" who used the country's Charter of Rights to rewrite legislation. In April, 1999, the Supreme Court overturned Judge McClung's ruling in the case of Vriend and ordered the Alberta government to include protection for gays in its human rights code.

The decision of the Supreme Court of Canada in the Ewanchuk case was delivered late in February, 1999, almost five years after the fact. The

Supreme Court reversed the decisions of the lower courts and convicted Ewanchuk in a unanimous decision, sending the case back to the original trial judge for sentencing. The Court ruled quite unequivocally that,

> The trial record conclusively establishes that the accused's persistent and increasingly serious advances constituted a sexual assault for which he had no defence...The trial judge relied on the defence of implied consent. This was a mistake of law as no such defence is available in assault cases in Canada.

How is it that a trial judge and appeals court can find that a woman who explicitly says no on four occasions, was actually implying consent? Supreme Court Justice Claire L'Heureux-Dubé wrote in a concurring opinion for herself and Justice Charles Gonthier, that it was not an error of law but rape myths which were responsible. "This error does not derive from the findings of fact but from mythical assumptions that when a woman says 'no' she is really saying 'yes,' 'try again,' or 'persuade me.'

> Myths of rape include the view that women fantasize about being rape victims; that women mean 'yes' even when they say 'no'; that any woman could successfully resist a rapist if she really wished to; that the sexually experienced do not suffer harms when raped (or at least suffer lesser harms than the sexually 'innocent'); that women often deserve to be raped on account of their conduct, dress, and demeanour; that rape by a stranger is worse than one by an acquaintance. Stereotypes of sexuality include the view of women as passive, disposed submissively to surrender to the sexual advances of active men, the view that sexual love consists in the 'possession' by a man of a woman, and that heterosexual sexual activity is paradigmatically penetrative coitus.[4]

L'Heureux-Dubé and Gonthier commented that, "Complainants should be able to rely on a system free from myths and stereotypes, and on a judiciary whose impartiality is not compromised by these biased assumptions," and then she proceeded to deconstruct and critique the decision by Justice John

McClung of the appeal court, mentioned above. McClung pointed to Barbara's clothing, and noted that "she was the mother of a six-month-old baby and that, along with her boyfriend, she shared an apartment with another couple." L'Heureux-Dubé wondered why he would do this. "Could it be to express that the complainant is not a virgin? Or that she is a person of questionable moral character because she is not married and lives with her boyfriend and another couple?" According to this logic, Barbara's refusal "cannot be taken as seriously as if she were a girl of 'good' moral character."

As for McClung's contention that Ewanchuk had "romantic intentions," L'Heureux-Dubé and Gonthier commented: "This is hardly a scenario one would characterize as reflective of 'romantic intentions.' It was nothing more than an effort by Ewanchuk to engage the complainant sexually, not romantically." McClung's use of phrases such as "clumsy passes" and not-exactly "chivalric behaviour" served to "minimize the importance of the accused's conduct," wrote L'Heureux- Dubé. His characterization of the attack as "far less criminal than hormonal," would excuse anyone who can't control hormonal urges.

L'Heureux-Dubé said McClung's exhortation to Barbara and other women that they use the "less litigious" route of a slap or knee to the groin, demonstrates that rape "is the only crime that has required the victim to resist physically in order to establish nonconsent."

L'Heureux-Dubé indicated that despite changes to the criminal code which attempted to eradicate reliance on such myths and stereotypes, they persist. "It is part of the role of this Court to denounce this kind of language, unfortunately still used today, which not only perpetuates archaic myths and stereotypes about the nature of sexual assaults but ignores the law."

HOW *THE NATIONAL POST* SAW THINGS

In its first news article the next day, The National Post described Justice L'Heureux-Dubé as "the court's feminist." It said L'Heureux-Dubé and Justice Beverly McLachlin wrote separate opinions "scolding Judge McClung," though McLachlin "was less vehement than Judge L'Heureux- Dubé." Although *The Post* did mention briefly in the article that L'Heureux- Dubé wrote, "in an opinion supported by Judge Charles Gonthier," the opinion was otherwise treated as though L'Heureux- Dubé was its sole author. Even the headline indicated that "*Women* justices rebuke male judge."[5] And the first paragraph stated that "The Supreme Court's two women justices gave an unusual dressing down yesterday to a justice of the Alberta Court of Appeal for making several bold comments about a young sex assault victim."

It is important to note that this omission was consistent throughout the media coverage of the decision and its aftermath. Justice L'Heureux-Dubé was singled out as "the court's feminist," for criticism over a unanimous decision by the court, and despite the fact that her concurring opinion was co-authored by a male judge. Additionally, Justice Beverly McLachlin, who would later become Chief Justice, concurred with L'Heureux-Dubé and Gonthier, writing, "I also agree with Justice L'Heureux-Dubé that stereotypical assumptions lie at the heart of what went wrong in this case." For the media and in particular *The National Post*, it was necessary to isolate and concentrate on L'Heureux-Dubé, in order to portray this decision as a product of ill-considered ideological feminism, instead of the clear-headed, logical decision that it was.

McClung also wrote a brief letter to *The National Post*, which it ran that first day, along with another story quoting from the letter and highlighting the dispute between L'Heureux-Dubé and McClung, including a sidebar which listed "he says" and "she says" points. McClung accused L'Heureux-Dubé of a "graceless slide into personal invective" in her opinion, (an accusation *The Post* put into the headline) stating that this "allows some response." He went on to add that the "personal convictions of the judge, delivered again from her judicial chair, could provide a plausible explanation for the disparate (and growing) number of male suicides being reported in the Province of Quebec." (Dubé's husband, a professor at Laval, committed suicide in 1978, and her only son died of a mysterious virus in 1994).[6] The next day *The Post* ran a feature article on L'Heureux-Dubé, calling her a "loner," and quoting one professor to the effect that she is "isolated at one edge of the court."

"Her friends include a roster of feminists," the article said, and listed some examples.[7]

The next day, the papers ran a story about the "split" amongst federal MPs, over whether Justice McClung should be brought before the Canadian Judicial Council, over his remarks about Justice L'Heureux-Dubé. The headline in *The Post* included the Reform party's position backing "judges right to speak out," but omitted the position of Liberal and NDP members, who wanted McClung censured.[8]

The Post and McClung added insult to injury with an interview the next day, in which McClung said the assault victim "was not lost on her way home from the nunnery." He said the victim has been "portrayed as a wide-eyed little girl who didn't know what was happening to her. Well, come on, now." McClung said he was unaware that L'Heureux-Dubé's husband died in a suicide, and that he was just poking a little tongue-in-cheek fun at "my friend Claire." *The Post* described his vitriol as "a rebuttal" of the Supreme Court decision, and gave his position further play. McClung "said it was wrong for the Supreme Court to convict Steve Ewanchuk because the Crown never disproved that his 17-year-old victim consented to his advances." McClung said, "One of the fundamental tenets of the criminal law is that the accused is to be punished for what he intended, and that didn't happen in this case." Of course, that was throughly dealt with in the decision.

Obviously, McClung doesn't get it. His response to the decision by L'Heureux-Dubé and Gonthier demonstrates that he positively oozes the sexist and stereotypical values to which they referred. He was merely proving their point! All nine members of the Supreme Court, seven men and two women, made it clear that these views will not be tolerated. As Justice Beverly McLachlin noted in her own concurring decision: "On appeal, the idea also surfaced that if a woman is not modestly dressed, she is deemed to consent. Such stereotypical assumptions find their roots in many cultures, including our own. They no longer, however, find a place in Canadian law."

In *The Post* story, Kathleen Mahoney, a law professor at the University of Calgary (described as "a friend of Justice L'Heureux- Dubé") was quoted criticizing McClung. "I've never seen anything like this in my lifetime, in any court anywhere. I've seen judges make some fairly intemperate comments, but I've never seen this sort of personal attack. I hope a complaint is made with the Canadian Judicial Council."[9]

A story followed in which Thomas Berger, a one-time B.C. Supreme Court justice, said McClung "owes both an explanation and an apology." Granted, McClung didn't know about L'Heureux-Dubé's husband's suicide. "But the question remains, how could anyone make a connection between her judgments and the male suicide rate in Quebec? That is incomprehensible to the point of absurdity." Mr. Berger said Judge McClung was likely suffering from "wounded vanity" and was "clouded by resentment" when he took the unprecedented step of publicly belittling Judge L'Heureux-Dubé's opinion, the article said.

"If every judge who was reversed wrote a letter criticizing the court that reversed him, *The National Post* would be flooded with mail," Mr. Berger said. "Writing this letter was altogether inappropriate. It is too bad that the judge didn't show it to one or two of his colleagues before he sent it off. I'm sure his colleagues would have said, 'Oh, for God's sake, don't be an idiot.' "[10]

It's at this point that *The Post* weighed in furiously with its own editorial view. Although Judge McClung "violated judicial etiquette" in his letter, *The Post* said Justice L'Heureux-Dubé was "disingenuous" for taking "his words out of context" and "abusing her position to launch a sanctimonious attack" against McClung. Of course, McClung himself proved with his subsequent statements that his words were not taken out of context at all. *The Post* described the decision as "contorted legalese," and as a classic example of "ideologically twisted logic," and as "a feminist indictment of an entire sex."

There is little dispute that unwanted groping took place. But did Ewanchuk have reasonable grounds for believing the complainant had consented to his sexual advances? In the past, even feminists agreed that only those accused who actually intended harm from their wrongful acts were guilty...[the court] denied a defence based on a mistaken belief in a woman's consent.[11]

Well, speaking of twisted logic. Which syllable in the word "NO!", repeated four times, does *The Post* not comprehend? And if Ewanchuk really believed he had Barbara's consent, after all that, then why, when he had finally given up his attack on her, did he attempt to bribe her with the $100 bill, and ask her not to tell anyone about it? The point is this: under the law, the onus was on Ewanchuk to obtain Barbara's explicit consent for any sexual contact. He didn't, and despite this, he persisted in his sexual assault. Regardless of what myths and stereotypes appeal court judge John McClung was operating under, Barbara's clothing that day and her grudging acquiescence in entering the trailer and massaging Ewanchuk's shoulders, do not constitute consent, implied or otherwise. And why, one might ask, is *The National Post* so intent on coming to the defence of a convicted rapist? Ewanchuk personally is of no interest to *The Post*. But McClung, the neocon judge, is. So too are men's rights, however wrong. So it is important for *The Post* to tip the scales in favour of McClung and against 'dangerous feminists' like L'Heureux-Dubé. But more on *The Post's* reasons later.

The Post attempted to portray the decision as absurd: "She must give explicit verbal consent—'yes'—or be held to be saying 'no.' (This might pose a problem if either party is deaf.)" Finally, *The Post* argued (inaccurately) that the decision went above and beyond the Criminal Code, and lobbied for parliament to do something about it. "The legislature was not then prepared to subscribe to the Court's radical feminism, and it should now correct it."

Columnist Lorne Gunter provided his view, that McClung's bad manners had distracted us from the heart of the matter: Justice L'Heureux-Dubé's "judicial feminism," the high court's "legal sophistry," and its "bad law and twisted precedent."

[Y]et again, the Supreme Court has swallowed whole feminist definitions of sex and rape...For feminists, sex must be as black and white as contract law and probably as much fun. The male…must have in his possession a signed consent form from the female before proceeding in a respectful and fully protected manner, in a place and at a time of prior mutual consent. That's not sex, it's surgery.[12]

The next day, Judge McClung issued an apology to Justice L'Heureux-Dubé, in the form of a press release, saying that his letter to *The Post* critiquing L'Heureux-Dubé was "an overwhelming error." In the story on this, we learned that the letter was in fact in response to a phone call to McClung from Shawn Ohler, a *National Post* reporter, looking for his reaction to the Supreme Court decision. We learned from a judicial "expert" that McClung's condition would stand him in good stead with the Canadian Judicial Council, which received several complaints against McClung. We also learned from *The Post's* editor-in-chief Kenneth White that McClung called Shawn Ohler, the reporter, leaving a message on his voice mail to thank him for "the balanced coverage" *The National Post* gave the story.[13] And, we learned all this in yet another story by Shawn Ohler.

"A MOST GRACIOUS MAN"

When a neo-con such as John McClung thinks he's getting "balanced" reporting, we know we're in trouble. Sure enough, the "balanced" story by Ohler the next day carried this headline: "Groundswell of support rises for embattled McClung: Respected by lawyers: Supporters fear witch hunt against 'gracious' judge." Guess which supporter Ohler went to for the quote about the "gracious" judge McClung? Why, Senator Anne Cools, who found him to be humble, sensitive, generous, indeed "a great luminary" who was subjected to a witch hunt. McClung's apology to L'Heureux-Dubé, is revealing, Cools said.

> It reveals that Judge McClung is a most gracious man, isn't he? And very, very humble. I'm deeply touched by his sensitivity and his generosity. I have great respect for John Wesley McClung and I would be concerned if he is submitted to any mean-spirited witch hunt. I don't

believe that he meant anything untoward. He is one of the great luminaries of the Canadian judicial system.[14]

No voice is given here to the question of why such a gracious and sensitive man would make the cruel remarks that he did about the victim of sexual assault, during the appeal and yet again, later in an interview, disparaging her appearance and her innocence, blaming her for the assault by a convicted rapist. Or, the incredible remark about Quebec women such as Justice L'Heureux-Dubé, driving their husbands to suicide by virtue of their feminist views. McClung is one of their own in high places, and he must be protected from persecution, and so the forces of vindication and absolution convened.

It is interesting to note the metamorphosis that Justice L'Heureux-Dubé's decision has undergone, in the span of a week. On February 26 the woman reporter assigned to the story for *The Post,* Janice Tibbetts, wrote: "Judge L'Heureux-Dubé issued a particularly scathing rebuke, vigorously dissecting each of several observations Judge McClung made last year."[15] Even the original story by Tibbetts and Shawn Ohler said L'Heureux-Dubé had " sharply criticized" McClung, while "dissecting" his decision. By March 3, Shawn Ohler wrote that "Justice L'Heureux- Dubé took the unusual step of belittling the Alberta jurist's Appeal Court ruling in a separate opinion." Hence, a 'scathing rebuke which vigorously dissected the opinion,' became 'the unusual step of belittling McClung.' It's easy to see how this portrayal served to justify McClung's behaviour, and to help him in his defence before the Canadian Judicial Council.

GIVING CREDIT WHERE IT'S DUE

Of course, resident antifeminist Donna Laframboise had to go on the record with her views on the matter, March 3. She starts off promisingly, but then backslides, arguing that no-doesn't-mean-no.

In a culture in which promiscuous males are called studs while promiscuous females are considered sluts, women have an incentive to be less than forthright, to say "no" when what they're really thinking

118

is "maybe" or "let's wait and see." Many women do mean it when they say "no." But others are buying time while they make up their minds, and still others enjoy being pursued.

Laframboise adopts a peculiar position on the "crinolines" point, caustically observing that "while no woman deserves to be raped because of what she's wearing, it's naive in the extreme to deny that our attire transmits sexual cues." Just what the role was of these "sexual cues" such as shorts and a T-shirt, in the sexual assault, Laframboise doesn't say. She goes on to defend the defendant for not committing violent rape, taking her typical men's rights position, yet again demonstrating that everyone with a degree in women's studies is not a feminist.

> With four previous sexual assault convictions on his record, the accused in this case is nobody's idea of a poster boy. But although the Supreme Court has convicted him of sexual assault in this instance, it must be stressed that the man did not violently rape this complainant. She testified that she said "no" on three occasions, after which he ceased his groping, lifted himself off of her, and put his penis back in his pants. Rather than initiate forcible intercourse, the accused backed off. He then tried to clumsily compensate her by giving her $100, and later called her at home to inquire after her well being. But the Supreme Court gives him no credit for finally getting the message. Indeed, throughout the judgment, sexual assault complainants receive every benefit of the doubt while accused persons are given no quarter.[16]

Actually, the Supreme Court did give him credit for "finally getting" the message: he was only convicted of sexual assault rather than rape. Note how Laframboise uses the term "clumsily compensate," to portray this in a positive manner, just as Judge McClung used "clumsy passes" toward the same ends. Similarly, Ewanchuk's attemp to cover his behind with a phone call, becomes, "to inquire about her well being."

Next into the fray was *National Post* columnist George Jonas, a particularly reactionary columnist who is a former husband of Barbara Amiel. This time Jonas was writing a column in the *Toronto Sun*, with the rather subdued headline: "The Canadian Matriarchy's Reign of Terror." (Jonas aside, on the whole, *Toronto Sun* columnists and writers, including Peter Worthington, actually were more progressive on this issue than was *The Post*).[17] Jonas said that historically 'no' has always meant 'no,' and that if there is a change with this landmark decision, "it must mean that 'yes' means 'no,' " and that any woman can change her mind at any time and charge a man with rape. According to Jonas, L'Heureux-Dubé chose "to read [McClung] the riot act about not being in tune with feminist thinking about human behaviour."

> Our courts adopt feminist notions by now as if they were scientific facts, with any contrary view dismissed by calling it 'archaic,' 'myth,' or 'stereotype'…Feminism in Canada has acquired the status of state religion. It's a theocracy in which the matriarchy's high priestesses impose and celebrate their rule in government, academia and the judicial system. The primary purpose of the laws of sexual assault is [sic] no longer to protect the vulnerable—or even specifically women—but to serve as an instrument of the matriarchy's reign of terror.[18]

And they accuse women of hysteria.

REAL WOMEN TO THE RESCUE

That same day, over at *The National Post*, Shawn Ohler was reporting on new demands by a national women's group for the resignation of Justice L'Heureux-Dubé, because of her demeaning and belittling treatment of Judge McClung. REAL Women of Canada's founder and vice-president Gwen Landolt said,

> [L'Heureux-Dubé] particularly named Judge McClung and tore him to pieces in a very humiliating and demeaning way. You may dis-

agree with him, but it is your duty as a Supreme Court judge to treat him with dignity and respect. She has used her position to humiliate a judge who dared to disagree with her personal opinion, and she should therefore be removed.[19]

Of interest is the way in which REAL women handled the minor problem of Justice Charles Gonthier, who also concurred in the decision. To his credit, Ohler asked REAL women about this, in one of only two instances in which the point came up, referring to him as one who "also signed Judge L'Heureux-Dubé's opinion."

Supreme Court Justice Charles Gonthier also signed Judge L'Heureux-Dubé's opinion, but REAL Women has no quarrel with him, Mrs. Landolt said. "We have pretty well accepted that he is in the feminist camp, but he is more even-handed. And he did not write the decision. That is the difference. He just sort of tagged along saying, 'Yeah, yeah, she's right.' "

Of course, this is nonsense, but it passed unquestioned in *The Post*.

In what was later called an example of "breathtaking hyperbole," criminal lawyer Edward Greenspan was next on the attack. Whatever his success in the courtroom, Greenspan managed to outdo Jonas, (with whom he has written a book) and probably did more damage than good to McClung's case. As the saying goes, with friends like these, who needs enemies? Greenspan argued that the position of Supreme Court Justice doesn't give anyone the right to " publicly humiliate, heap scorn, ridicule or cause enormous pain" to a lower court judge. They don't have the right "to pull a lower court judge's pants down in public and paddle him." Justices shouldn't "say mean, gratuitous, and terrible things..."

By labelling Judge McClung, in effect, the male chauvinist pig of the century, the chief yahoo from Alberta, the stupid, ignorant, ultimate sexist male jerk, Judge L'Heureux-Dubé did an unnecessary and mean-spirited thing. It was undignified and very wrong.

121

FEMINISTS UNDER THE BED

Justice L'Heureux-Dubé "drew first blood." She "was intemperate, showed a lack of balance, and a terrible lack of judgment," she poured "salt in the wound" and "step[ped] on the lower court judge's face." Finally, said Greenspan of L'Heureux-Dubé, "Let the record show that she is not a very nice person." Ironically, L'Heureux-Dubé's rebuke of McClung paled next to Greenspan's delirious attack on L'Heureux-Dubé.

But this was just the warmup for Greenspan's main target: the feminists.

> It is clear that the feminist influence has amounted to intimidation, posing a potential danger to the independence of the judiciary. I deplore any attempt to use the Canadian Judicial Council as an agent of the women's movement, through the filing of complaints against judges whose remarks do not accord with the feminist world view. Feminists have entrenched their ideology in the Supreme Court of Canada and have put all contrary views beyond the pale. I predicted a long time ago a judicial embracing of the feminist perspective. But to call for Judge McClung's removal or censure means the feminists and their fellow travellers have created such a repressive and authoritarian world that certain words are not only unacceptable, but now constitute misconduct. The feminist perspective has hijacked the Supreme Court of Canada and now feminists want to throw off the bench anyone who disagrees with them. That no one in academia or legal circles has stood up for Judge McClung to date is shocking.[20]

One feminist out of nine members of the Supreme Court has posed a threat to the independence of the judiciary!!! Greenspan, who defended former Nova Scotia premier Gerald Regan against sexual assault charges, must see monsters under his bed at night as well. What about the threat to more than half of the population posed by the abundance of sexist men like McClung on the court? No problem for Greenspan in his virulent antifeminism!

The Post allowed a column to be run in response to Greenspan, by Kim Buchanan, a staff lawyer, and Carissima Mathen, the director of litigation with the Women's Legal Education and Action Fund (LEAF). LEAF presented a brief to the Supreme Court in the Ewanchuk case. Buchanan and Mathen pointed out that a bonnet and crinolines are not "the only appropriate attire for a woman who wishes to attend a job interview without signaling sexual availability to the interviewer." They reiterated the fact that Ewanchuk repeatedly touched the complainant sexually, escalating to more invasive contact every time she said 'no.' While Judge McClung did not see this as a crime, they wrote, the Supreme Court has made it clear: "Canadian law does not require that a woman engage in a fist-fight with every man who wants to have sex with her, merely to demonstrate she really means it when she says 'no.' " While Greenspan claimed the decision shows "feminists" have "hijacked" the Supreme Court, Justice John Major wrote, and all nine judges agreed, "Society is committed to protecting the personal integrity, both physical and psychological, of every individual. Having control over who touches one's body, and how, lies at the core of human dignity and autonomy." Justice Major also held that both women and men are entitled to "the peace of mind of knowing that their bodily integrity and autonomy in deciding when and whether to participate in sexual activity will be respected."

Buchanan and Mathen asked, "Is this the reasoning of feminists run amok?"

> It was perfectly proper for Justice L'Heureux-Dubé to debunk the myth that, if a woman is not a virgin, she is less believable, deserves to be assaulted, is not harmed by sexual assault, or is more likely to consent to sex...Mr. Greenspan's inflammatory rhetoric aside, the Ewanchuk decision was no revolution. The Supreme Court simply confirmed the law that was on the books already (but the Alberta courts had ignored): Every person is entitled to decide whether, when, and with whom they wish to be sexually involved. Submission out of fear is not consent to sex. Every person is entitled to have his or her "no" respected. A woman's dress or sexual history do not make it alright to sexually assault her.[21]

Now, presumably those who work for *The National Post* also read that newspaper, and would have seen this column. But this was not the end of the matter.

Columnist Christie Blatchford went on to conclude that, "Judge McClung wasn't adhering to archaic beliefs and rape myths, not in my book, anyway. He used impolitic language to speak common sense."[22] And, of course, Barbara Amiel leapt in that same day, in a mammoth 2500- word column headlined, "Feminists, fascists, and other radicals: Claire L'Heureux-Dubé opposes the ideas for which we fought WWII and the Cold War."

Amiel began by defending McClung, saying his response was justified because "[L'Heureux-Dubé] wrote a bully's attack on him," which was "unprecedented in its discourteous, ad hominem attack upon a fellow judge." Having said this, Amiel then went on, incredibly, to write of L'Heureux-Dubé, that: "she is living beyond her intellectual means. She doesn't really understand what she is saying, or its consequences...she is an example of the singular kindness Canada shows in giving lesser minds a role in society." This attack on L'Heureux-Dubé exceeded the one by McClung, or even Greenspan. From there, her column deteriorated into what can only be described as the maniacal rant implied by its headline. Amiel tells us, conspiratorially, that while the debate on this matter still rages, "an ominous silence clothes the key issue." You can guess what it is.

In fact, for a very long time now, feminism has had absolutely nothing to do with equality for women—quite the opposite. It is now a movement whose name has been hijacked by radicals fundamentally opposed to all our institutions and heritage...By now our institutions have been so affected by radical feminism that it is hard to know how to countermand their grip on our lives...They believe that women have a different reality, and that all our institutions must be changed and fundamentally altered to respond to that reality. Far from creating equality, such feminists are exclusionary. They wish to create a new privileged caste, namely the matriarchy...These feminists are, in fact, promoting gender wars...Like all ideologues, they have structured a universe in which everything proves whatever they wish it to prove and it is all used to structure a matriarchical [sic] system in which they will be able to wield almost unchecked power through intimidation, the establishment of standards and structures of morality that suit their ideology and function to their own benefit...Though small in number, they occupy influential positions and have formidable weapons with which to intimidate...Ultimately, these feminists permit the state, on the basis of promoting various feminist aims, to encroach further and further on the autonomy of the family. Here is an alliance indeed: a power-grab by a statist matriarchy.[23]

It is important to note that aside from being a columnist and partner to press baron Conrad Black, from 1996 to 2000—including the time when she wrote this—Amiel was the vice-president responsible for editorial and news content for all of the Southam newspapers.

SUBSTANTIVE EQUALITY

In a column she submitted in response to Amiel, law professor Kathleen Mahoney referred to the two visions of equality mentioned by Amiel: formal equality, with which Amiel agrees, and substantive equality, which Amiel sees as a scourge. Formal equality treats all people the same under the law. Substantive equality seeks to ensure the impact of laws is fair. Feminists, who stand for greater substantive equality and human rights, are "lightening rods for [Amiel's] anger." Professor Mahoney said that Amiel's writing "fits into a pattern of backlash that can be traced to the mediaeval ages," when women seeking equality were burned at the stake as witches. At the beginning of the 20th century, suffragettes were attacked by the press, religious leaders and academics "who said they would be the cause of infertility, crises in the family, and increased divorce rates." In the 1930s, feminists promoting birth control were attacked as "evil, selfish and immoral and the cause of insanity, tuberculosis, diabetes, and cancer in women who practise birth control." Regarding formal versus substantive equality, Professor Mahoney says "the debate is over."

> What Ms. Amiel doesn't seem to know is that all provincial legislatures embrace substantive equality in their human rights legislation and Parliament constitutionally enshrined substantive equality in 1982. Formal equality was also replaced by substantive equality in the common law by an all-male Supreme Court of Canada in 1985. In 1989, substantive equality was affirmed as a fundamental principle of constitutional law. Justice McIntyre, who led the [Supreme] court in the landmark case, is hardly a radical feminist.[24]

Mahoney pointed out that Supreme Court Justice McIntyre, in rejecting formal equality, (Amiel's preference), said "it is a seriously flawed concept that could justify the Nuremberg laws of Adolf Hitler, and was used to justify the segregation of Blacks in the United States through the separate but equal doctrine."

At this point, on March 15, *The Post* also ran an unsolicited rebuttal to Greenspan's column, by Justice Alex Kozinski of the Federal Court of Appeals in California, to which he was appointed by President Ronald Reagan in 1985. Kozinski begins by noting that Greenspan's diatribe is truly remarkable in that it says nothing about L'Heureux-Dubé's judgement. "He neither quotes it, nor describes it, nor even identifies what about it he finds offensive—other than to attribute to its author a mindless feminist ideology." Kozinski clarifies why L'Heureux-Dubé had to name McClung, which she was criticized for doing. He said she had to identify him rather than referring to the Court of Appeal judgement, "because no other member of his own court signed on to Judge McClung's quaint views." Rather than delivering a belittling attack, as charged, Kozinski says that L'Heureux-Dubé "Calmly, and without rancor" addressed each of Judge McClung's points "and refuted them." Kozinski paraphrased and summarized her points:

When a woman dresses in shorts, appropriate to the weather, this is not an invitation for groping by perfect strangers.

Not being a virgin makes the complainant no less worthy of belief, nor is it implied consent to have sexual relations with every willing male.

By saying "no" and "I am very scared" the complainant was not inviting the accused to climb on top of her, fondle private parts of her anatomy and touch her with his penis.

Responding to "hormonal" urges is not a defence to sexual assault charges, or else most sexual assaults would be excusable.

A woman is not required to insult, slap or kick her way out of an intimidating situation involving a man twice her age and weight.

Kozinski asked, "Are these the examples of the 'feminist world view' that Mr. Greenspan complains so bitterly about?" Rather than hurling invective at McClung, as Greenspan and others would have us believe, Kozinski says L'Heureux-Dubé's judgement "neither berates nor chastises him," but instead she argues that his approach of blaming the victim doesn't reflect "contemporary notions of how men and women should relate in a civilized society."

Confronted by McClung's inappropriate language, what was L'Heureux-Dubé to do, Kozinski asked? Remain mute? Or does she have a duty to "repudiate the language and the sentiments behind it?"

If a lower court judge were to say that, "The complaining witness deserved to be robbed because all Jewish shopkeepers cheat their customers," the Supreme Court would surely feel obligated to point out that this reflects invidious stereotypes, not reality. Why then was it wrong for Justice L'Heureux-Dubé to explain that by dressing in shorts and being a single mother, the complainant was not angling for sex during a job interview?[25]

The next day *The Post* ran a story about how Justice L'Heureux-Dubé allegedly fled a group of broadcast and print reporters, insisting she would make "no comment," after giving a speech to mark International Women's Day 1999. L'Heureux-Dubé's "hasty exit shortly before a question period began" was said by *The Post* to have "neatly sidestepped a potential ambush by a member of REAL Women."[26]

On March 10, John Fraser wrote a rambling and unfocussed essay of 1000 words in the Arts section, advising people to wait before writing letters in haste. He saw both parties, L'Heureux-Dubé and McClung, as being at fault. "If, in retrospect, they were given the chance to temper their words, I expect they would both do it."[27] I guess this is what passes for "balance" at *The Post.*

That same day, *The Post* ran an editorial questioning the integrity and independence of The Canadian Judicial Council, where it said, "conflicts of interest abound."

"If there can be no appearance of fairness whatsoever in the way we judge our judges, then we have not justice but arbitrary tyranny," *The Post* pontificated, setting up a ready-made excuse in case McClung was eventually reprimanded or removed, and also putting the Council on notice that it was under intense media scrutiny, (a kind of "publicity chill"). *The Post* pointed to Supreme Court Justice Jack Major as both a friend of Judge John McClung and a colleague of Justice L'Heureux- Dubé, and the one who wrote the Supreme Court decision. And it mentioned the Honourable Catherine Fraser, chief justice of Alberta, McClung's boss on the Alberta court and his "intellectual nemesis" according to *The Post.*[28]

Unfortunately for *The Post*, its assumptions about conflict of interest were groundless, as Justice Allan McEachern pointed out in a subsequent letter. As it turns out neither Major nor Fraser are even on the Judicial Council.[29]

GREENSPAN BACK ON THE ATTACK

The next day, *The Post* gave Edward Greenspan another 1600 words to respond to Justice Kozinski, to add to his earlier column of 1400 words. Aside from additional personal insults, belittling the time Kozinski had on his hands for writing on this matter (?) and clearly indicating that an American doesn't have a right to comment on Canadian affairs ("My initial reaction was, 'Yankee go home,' ") Greenspan dredges up more attacks on feminists and peppers his comments with a racist expression (italicized).

[Kozinski] misses why I am criticizing. When I chose to write on this subject, the National Council of Women and other feminist pressure groups *were on their way to mau mau* the Canadian Judicial Council, to censure, remove, or otherwise sanction Justice McClung, not for his intemperate letter for which he apologized and which was merely an excuse, but for his refusal to internalize feminist thought into his legal analysis. He had to go because of his refusal to accept feminist dogma.[30]

"Mau Mau" was a derogatory term given to a nationalist movement amongst the Kikuyu people of Kenya, in the 1950s.[31]

Kozinski's comparatively well-reasoned response came in a letter with a mere 840 words, on March 15, which concluded as follows:

Judge McClung's words thrust searing irons into the wounds the victim had already suffered. By calling Judge McClung on his hurtful language, Justice Claire L'Heureux-Dubé was saying that victims of sexual assault should not suffer yet again by having to endure public comments about their chastity, marital status, and other intimate aspects of their personal lives. This is not such an earth-shattering proposition. Canada, like other civilized countries, has already adopted this as the standard of behaviour in its courtrooms by passing strong rape shield laws that severely limit inquiry into a victim's private life. This was done by the people's elected representatives, not by out-of-control judicial feminists. It's a bit of a mystery to me why Mr. Greenspan and Judge McClung still believe this is controversial.[32]

I could find no further response from Greenspan.

The March 11 *National Post* carried a story about an attempt by the Alberta Crown Attorney's office to have Ewanchuk declared a dangerous offender, which would mean that he would receive an indeterminate sentence. The story mostly consisted of an interview with Ewanchuk's lawyer, Brian Beresh, who described his shock and that of his client, and his arguments why it would not be appropriate. There was a brief (and favourable to Ewanchuk) account of the assault, and Paul Bernardo was the only named example given of a dangerous offender.[33]

Two days later *The Post* reported that a national fathers' group had filed a complaint with the Canadian Judicial Council against Justice L'Heureux-Dubé and had vowed to file a complaint against all nine judges on the Supreme Court of Canada for their "feminist" slant in decisions that deny men access to children after divorce. The National Shared Parenting Association, a Toronto-based fathers' group which claims a national membership of about 1,000, was formed to lobby the government over its planned changes to child custody laws. "Justice L'Heureux-Dubé has made it clear on too many occasions that she is unable to separate her personal agenda from the duties of her appointment," said the letter of complaint.[34]

The next article described how a group of Alberta lawyers had begun a petition for standing before the Canadian Judicial Council, to ensure a "fair hearing" into the conduct of John McClung, due to concerns that the inquiry would be dominated by "special interest groups."[35]

Next, a story pointed to gender balance in the Alberta high court leading to a "schism." The story said that seven of 12 full-time justices in the Alberta high court are women, including chief justice Catharine Fraser. One "sinister" result, *The Post* said, is a "pronounced schism" on the court, especially between Fraser and McClung. The story described Fraser as "an extremely strong personality," and "aggressive" and "nervy." Fraser "has less of a conciliatory personality that her predecessor," and "is perhaps not the right person to bring a disparate group of people together," the story said. Judge McClung, on the other hand, whose decisions have "enraged countless interest groups," has the social values of "a traditional old gentleman," according to professor Chris Levy, a University of Calgary law professor. "That stance often bristles against the proudly feminist bent of Judge Fraser, Levy said.[36]

One does not have to read between the lines here to see that the 'feminist' chief justice Fraser is being blamed for the schism on the court.

That same day, *The Post* went to bat for the record of the Alberta court, misinterpreting the statistics in a study of reversals by the Supreme Court. The headline read: "Top Alberta court not as contrary as believed," and the opening paragraphs read as follows:

> The Alberta Court of Appeal's renowned resistance to judicial activism and anti-Charter bent may in fact be a myth. A new study reveals its decisions are no more likely to be overturned by the country's top court than those of most other provincial appellate courts. Over the last eight years, 48% of the constitutional cases from the Alberta Court of Appeal that have gone before the Supreme Court of Canada have been reversed, a figure that is only slightly ahead of the average reversal rate of 40%.[37]

Hence, the average reversal rate for all of the provinces including Alberta was 40%, and Alberta's own average was *twenty percent higher than average,* at 48%. I'd call that a significant difference, especially when compared to the 32% rate in Ontario, for example. (Remember, this is a complete census of decisions, rather than a partial sample).

AN EX-HUSBAND TO THE RESCUE

No longer satisfied writing on the issue for *The Toronto Sun,* George Jonas now wrote a 2050-word essay in *The Post,* responding to those who attacked Amiel and Greenspan. "Ms. Amiel and Mr. Greenspan are my friends and one-time co-authors," he admitted, but failed to mention that he was once married to Ms. Amiel, and that she hired him to write for Southam and *The Post.* Actually, he says he writes not to defend them as they are perfectly capable, but only because, "There's a limit on what I can tolerate supporters of the matriarchy saying, unchallenged, in print." Jonas begins by stating that law professor Kathleen Mahoney is being disingenuous as she really wishes to substitute "inequality" (which is what she means by "substantive equality") for "formal equality" in order to "prove the feminist point that equality equals inequality."

He clarifies his own (and Amiel's) position, supplying the missing link between feminism and fascism: "under the pressure of statist forces, including radical feminists, Canada has snatched the blindfold from the Goddess of Justice. This precisely is the problem. This is how our system is coming to resemble fascism and communism."

"You cannot treat people differently to achieve equality for the same reason you can't make an iron hoop out of wood: It's a contradiction in terms," Jonas writes. He refers back to Mahoney's example of the use of wheelchair ramps for the handicapped. Mahoney wrote that "disabled people are entitled to be treated differently in order to achieve equality."

> I was waiting for Prof. Mahoney to trot out the wheelchair ramps, and she didn't disappoint me...Even if one accepted that one person's disability puts another person under a legal obligation to build ramps for him—a gigantic "if"—the illustration breaks down when it comes to races and genders. In what respect does Prof. Mahoney regard races as crippled? What precisely are the moral or intellectual disabilities of women for which they need to be treated differently, in Prof. Mahoney's view?

What Jonas would have wheelchair users do if ramps were not built for them, he doesn't say. But I believe the point here, which Mahoney did not elaborate in her brief piece, is that if someone or some group has been disadvantaged, then merely granting them "equality" after the fact is inadequate. As far as race is concerned, a good example would be culturally biased "intelligence" or "scholastic achievement" tests. There's little good in treating all test scores "equally," regardless of race or class, if the bias already has been built into the testing. As for gender, slim and petite Barbara

McDonald was at a physical disadvantage given that she was in the bulky, ex-con Ewanchuk's trailer. Because of this physical disadvantage, as with the disadvantages of fear from real or perceived violence, and power relations (prospective employer vs. employee), it was all the more incumbent on Ewanchuk to avoid sexual assault charges by clearly and unambiguously obtaining consent before making advances. As a convicted rapist, no one should be more conscious of this than him.

But Jonas, like the others at *The Post*, either doesn't understand or won't accept the simple concepts involved here. He demonstrates it as follows, in weighing the question whether it is Barbara or Ewanchuk who is the victim:

> To determine this question fairly—who is the victim—does it help to consider whether a complainant was scantily clad? Does it help to consider whether she was an unwed teenage mother? Well, in a mail fraud case it probably doesn't; in a sexual assault case maybe it does. It depends on the totality of the circumstances…it's sheer doctrinaire, ideological nonsense to say that a trier of fact who considers dress, background, or demeanor in sexual assault "perpetuates archaic myths and stereotypes."[00]

Of course, it's illegal to consider the victim's "background," in terms of previous sexual experience, which is what McClung was doing, and what Jonas is defending. As for dress, well, it doesn't matter if someone is naked—that doesn't mean you can assault or rape them. That's why dress is irrelevant and McClung was out of line.

The writings of Jonas, Amiel, Laframboise and others at *The Post* consist almost entirely of hyperbole and invective, and are devoid of reasoning. Feminism run amok is their evil Satan, and is almost entirely of their own creation. Their method is to take a kernel of truth such as a Supreme Court decision, and then manufacture hysterical plots and scenarios, without a shred of evidence. Here is Jonas again:

Normally feminists not only regard their ideas as universal truth, but call on the authorities for the removal of anyone who disagrees with them. They usually demand human rights commissions or judicial councils to censure their opponents or fire them from their jobs. It's one of several reasons why some people, myself included, have tended to confuse the matriarchy—if "confuse" is the word—with fascists and communists.

ONE HAND WASHES THE OTHER

Next, with utterly meagre evidence, *The Post* pointed to L'Heureux- Dubé's "firm hand and feminist perspective" as being "expected to guide" an imminent Supreme Court ruling on the issue of a spouse's financial obligation to a former spouse who falls ill, in the Bracklow case. Here is the type of paltry proof provided for this claim, indeed this entire story, which again reviewed L'Heureux-Dubé's role in the McClung and Ewanchuk controversies.

> "Judge L'Heureux-Dubé has a lot of interest in family law matters and a very good understanding of those matters," says Roxanne Mykitiuk, a professor at York University's Osgoode Hall who specializes in family law. "I'm sure she'll take a lead role, even if it's not in writing, but in trying to influence her colleagues."[39]

It turns out that the decision actually was written by Justice Beverly McLaughlin, and was "based on traditional views," which *The Post* said "surprises analysts." Analysts such as *The Post*, which had been spreading hype about feminist bogeywomen.[40]

Next, *The Post* reported on a call by Reform party leader Preston Manning, for a "review [of] high court rulings that run counter to the intent of federal laws," and for questioning of Supreme Court appointees by members of parliament, about "their qualifications and philosophies," based on the U.S. model.[41] This is a good example of the harmonious exchange between the right-wing press and right-wing parties. The press raises and hammers away at 'issues' and creates the 'groundswell' for a 'crisis,' and then the political party picks up the theme and continues the political battle in the forum of the legislature and, of course, the media. Of course, sometimes it's the politicians who begin the clamour. Other co-conspirators are involved in the dance, such as Gwen Landolt of REAL Women of Canada, as mentioned above. (Just as NDP leader Alexa McDonough complained to the Judicial Council of Canada about Judge McClung's comments about Justice L'Heureux-Dubé).

It's all part of *The Post's* campaign of furor over the alleged hijacking of the Supreme Court by the lone feminist L'Heureux-Dubé, in which Manning, Reform (now Alliance) and REAL Women were willing ideological collaborators.

By the beginning of April, some five weeks into the affair, *The Post* was now reporting what for them was the bad news that L'Heureux-Dubé had been cleared by the Judicial Council of any wrongdoing in her remarks about McClung contained in her opinion. Her language was "robust," but also "well within the ambit of the case," according to the panel of her peers. The complaint against L'Heureux-Dubé was brought by REAL Women, and Gwen Landolt was given a chance by *The Post* to re-state her case about the "demeaning personal invective" used by L'Heureux-Dubé, along with her argument that taxpayers shouldn't have to pay the salary of "a radical feminist who sits on the bench and used her position to promote her own personal agenda."[42]

Within a few days, *The Post* reported that REAL Women of Canada had accused L'Heureux-Dubé of "lying" to the Canadian Judicial Council while it considered a complaint against her. REAL said Justice L'Heureux-Dubé was Canadian vice-president of what it called a "feminist" body, the International Federation of Women Lawyers, (FIDA) in 1981, although she reportedly told the judicial body that she could recall no affiliation with the group. REAL Women was consequently renewing its demand for Justice L'Heureux-Dubé's removal. Why am I reminded of Joseph McCarthy here? "I am not now, and nor have I ever been, a member of the Communist Party." In this story, *The Post* reported that in dismissing REAL Women's initial complaint against Justice L'Heureux-Dubé, "the council said that, even if she was a member of FIDA, 'membership in such an association would not constitute judicial misconduct.' "[43]

This would appear to render her membership status a moot point, and it would also clearly render the story itself meaningless, for all intents and purposes. Such are the vagaries of news judgements. The story concluded: "Judge L'Heureux-Dubé could not be reached for comment last night." This is a striking comment, as she has not been quoted once in all of these stories, aside from the wording of her co-authored concurring decision in R. vs. Ewanchuk. Indeed, all of the Supreme Court justices refused to comment on any of these matters.

The next day *The Post* ran a front page story in which it said Justice L'Heureux-Dubé could be hurt by allegations that she lied; her credibility could be damaged. The story quoted Joseph Magnet, a law professor at the University of Ottawa.

> "It's a credibility thing, and it certainly doesn't help her credibility," he said. "Some people in the legal community think that she is not tremendously faithful to the law, that she stretches the law. Some people think she is too reckless in imposing her views, which are iconoclastic...This would lend a certain amount of fuel to those making those claims."[44]

The International Federation of Women Lawyers was established in 1944. According to *The Post's* own article, it is "a broad-based organization that advocates for the rights of women and children internationally." It works through the United Nations, "with the bulk of its focus on developing countries." Why membership in such a group would be something anyone would hide, is unexplained. Why the position of Canadian vice-president is anything other than a badge of honour, is a mystery. Yet, REAL Women and *The Post* appeared intent on branding Justice L'Heureux-Dubé with membership in a "feminist" organization, and fabricating an attempt on her part to hide the fact, when it appears to be a mere oversight. This gets blown up into "allegations she lied." Ironically, the story did go on to note that the point is indeed moot. "The point of her involvement appears to be moot as far as the official investigation goes, since the council ruled that even if she did belong to such a group, such membership 'would not constitute judicial misconduct.' " This should be rather obvious! All this was, of course, after the damage was already done to Justice L'Heureux-Dubé.

WHY JUSTICE L'HEUREUX-DUBÉ?

But there was more. Two days later, *The Post* ran another story indicating that L'Heureux-Dubé's membership in what it called "a woman's equality group" was "questionable," but "not necessarily a conflict of interest," according to "legal scholars."[45] In fact, the story quoted just one person: a political science professor at the University of Lethbridge. "It was not quite a conflict but it came close to the borderline," *The Post* got professor Peter McCormick to say. But he also went on to say that, "A judge having any executive position in a lawyers' organization is not a wise move. But to pull up a one-year episode from 17 years ago when she was two levels down from her current appointment is a stretch."

Of course, this means that the article could quite reasonably have been headlined: "Judicial expert says attack on L'Heureux-Dubé 'is a stretch.' " Instead, casual readers were now predominantly left with the impression that Justice L'Heureux-Dubé is a radical feminist with feminist friends and questionable memberships in feminist groups, that women like her are responsible for their husbands' suicides, that her calm and rational judgement was a feminist diatribe which amounts to an attack on men, and that she singled-out poor Judge McClung and belittled him, unfairly labelling him as "the male chauvinist pig of the century." Readers have also been told by *The Post* in a concerted campaign which has so far run on practically a daily basis from February 26 until April 10—about six weeks—that a complaint was laid against L'Heureux-Dubé before the Judicial Council, that she was exonerated due to judicial cronyism, that she has been accused of lying to the Judicial Council and covering up her involvement in a feminist organization, and that this behaviour is at least questionable and may put her in a conflict of interest, even though it took place 17 years previously. All of this because she is a feminist.

As we've seen, *The Post* did provide space on its letters page and in guest columns for some of those who wrote in to defend Justice L'Heureux-Dubé, and for criticism of the perspectives in the witch hunt undertaken across the board by virtually everyone writing for *The Post* itself. In this sense, the content of the newspaper at large was multilayered, there *were* oppositional readings available to the discerning reader. But these letters and columns were much fewer in number, much smaller in size, much less visible in terms of prominence, and were entirely written by amateurs, volunteering their time, as opposed to the paid professionals hired by *The Post*, who joined in this collective campaign to discredit Justice L'Heureux-Dubé, voluntarily or otherwise. Obviously, the only area in which the amateurs had an advantage was in the quality of their reasoning and the strength of their arguments, when compared to the mindless hyperbole and personal invective hurled by the hired hands at *The Post*.

Earlier, I indicated that convicted rapist Steve Ewanchuk is of no particular interest to the movers and shakers at *The Post*, but that defending Judge McClung and attacking Justice L'Heureux-Dubé was obviously important. But why? Is it just a personal vendetta against feminists? Evidently *The Post* does have a knee-jerk antifeminist perspective, but there is more to it than that. The reasoning surfaced in a news article written later in the year, in September. *The Post's* ownership and management was concerned that the activist Supreme Court was using the Canadian Charter of Rights and Freedoms as a tool in changing social policy. (Recall from above how, in his decision in the Delwin Vriend case which was later reversed by the Supreme Court, Judge McClung railed against "crusading...ideologically determined judges" who used the country's Charter of Rights to rewrite legislation). The story focussed predominantly on the changes to the Supreme Court wrought by the appointments made by Prime Minister Jean

Chretien, whose influence it said, would last for "centuries." Here's what the story by Janice Tibbetts said, in part.

> Appointments to the Supreme Court are under increasing scrutiny because of the impact the judges have on the everyday lives of Canadians, *handing down groundbreaking rulings on the most pressing social issues of the day, ranging from rights for gays and aboriginals to sex discrimination and child support*...A recent gay-rights ruling, for example, ordered Ontario to change its definition of spouse to include same-sex couples. The ruling is expected to result in the dismantling of hundreds of laws across the country that deny benefits, including pensions, to same-sex couples.[46]

So, *The Post's* real concern in all of this was not Justice L'Heureux-Dubé *per se*, but the progressive views generally held by feminists, and the fact that hard-won gains by the right, in promoting social and fiscal neo-conservatism, might be lessened or even undone by an activist and progressive court which would stand up for gays, women, visible minorities, *et cetera*. These concerns were not lessened later in 1999 when the first woman was named chief justice, Beverly McLachlin, and when another Francophone was named to replace retiring chief justice Antonio Lamer, leading to a Francophone majority on the court. As Francophones historically have held more progressive social views, these developments were greeted with alarm at *The Post*.[47]

Further evidence of the court's mildly-progressive nature and *The Post's* apprehension of this came in January 2001, when the newspaper reported the following:

> James Kelly, a political scientist at Brock University, has analyzed voting records of Supreme Court judges since the inception of the Charter of Rights and Freedoms through 1999. He finds that of all the judges to sit on the top bench since the adoption of the Charter, the current group...*are the most likely to support equality rights of minority groups, women, and aboriginal groups*.[48]

Indeed, later in 1999 Justice L'Heureux-Dubé was again attacked by *The Post* in an editorial and in columns, for her open position supporting gay rights. In October, in a speech, Justice L'Heureux-Dubé said Canadian law functions as an "anchor and a constraint" when it comes to non-traditional relationships. In an editorial response, *The Post* called for her to "recuse herself from the bench" on decisions pertaining to such matters, and worried that next brothers and sisters would be treated as couples. "Among other problems, court decisions that extend marriage benefits to same-sex couples open the doors to putting other dependent relationships, such as widowed brothers and sisters, on a par with marriage.[49]

A retired law professor from the University of Western Ontario, Ian Hunter, then wrote a column supporting *The Post's* editorial position. Quoting from public remarks made by L'Heureux-Dubé, to the effect that, "The unequal pay and job opportunities available to women, sexual and racial harassment and discrimination and hate crimes committed against gays and lesbians are just some of the problems that international human rights laws implore all citizens to confront." Hunter asked whether a lawyer appearing before the court on any of these issues could "anticipate an impartial hearing"? He thought not.[50] Heaven forbid that a lawyer defending someone who *supports* unequal pay for women, or racial harassment and discrimination, and hate crimes against gays and lesbians, should apprehend bias! Since all of these things are illegal, presumably everyone in society, benchers included, is against them and thus has the same potential apprehension of "bias" as Justice L'Heureux-Dubé.

Next at bat was Ted Morton, a political science professor at the University of Calgary, prominent Reform Party member, and Alberta senator-elect. Morton wrote in *The Post* that Justice L'Heureux-Dubé told a conference in London England that Canadian courts "are taking the lead in changing society's attitudes to same-sex partnerships." Someone in attendance quoted Justice L'Heureux-Dubé as saying, in the panel discussion that followed, that she was "an equality person. I hate discrimination. I'll do anything I can to achieve it [equality]. Go by the spirit of human rights. You can call it partiality. I call it [being] human." Morton condemned this as blatant "partiality," and said recusing herself from cases "hardly goes far enough. The facts in this case demand a sterner sanction."[51] Well, again, why anyone should be castigated for a belief in human rights and equality and opposition to discrimination, is simply beyond rational understanding. Unless, of course, it is one in a series of blind and furious and irrational attacks.

There is more to the saga of *The Post* and Justice L'Heureux-Dubé but for reasons of time and space, this will have to suffice. Steve Ewanchuk was eventually sentenced, in October, 2000, to one year in prison for sexual assault. In response to the 24 complaints filed against him, Judge John McClung was severely reprimanded by the Canadian Judicial Council, later in May, 1999, for his remarks about Justice L'Heureux-Dubé, but he was not removed from the bench. The council said it was "simply unacceptable conduct for a judge" to imply the victim wasn't a "nice girl" or that she could have fought off the accused with a "slap in the face" or a "well-placed knee." It also criticized him for telling a *National Post* reporter that the assault victim "was not lost on her way home from the nunnery."[52]

And so, Justice Claire L'Heureux-Dubé was right.

NOTES

1. Ritu Khullar, of the Women's Legal Education and Action Fund (LEAF), in an interview along with criminal defence lawyer Ian Scott, by Leslie Mckinnon of CBC TV's *The National Magazine*, "A case of consent," October 14, 1998.

2. This account is substantially drawn from the Supreme Court decision in this case, especially the concurring opinion of Justice Claire L'Heureux-Dubé and Justice J.J. Gonthier. See R. *v.* Ewanchuk, [1999] 1 S.C.R. 330, File No.: 26493. 1998: October 14; 1999: February 25, 2000. The complainant was a minor. The name Barbara McDonald is made up.

3. Lisa Gregoire, "No-means-no sexual assailant free until next court appearance in November," *The National Post*, September 1, 1999.

4. David Archard, *Sexual Consent*, Westview Press, Boulder, Colorado, 1998, p 131.

5. Janice Tibbetts, "Women justices rebuke male judge in sex-assault case," *The National Post*, February 26, 1999.

6. Janice Tibbetts and Shawn Ohler, "Judges clash over landmark sex-assault ruling: No definitely means no: Supreme Court judge castigated for 'graceless slide into personal invective,' *The National Post*, February 26, 1999.

7. Janice Tibbetts, "Supreme Court's great dissenter,"*The National Post*, February 27, 1999.

8. Robert Fife, "MPs split over censuring McClung: Reform backs judge's right to speak out, *The National Post*, February 27, 1999.

9. Shawn Ohler, "Judge reiterates belief that teen wasn't assaulted: Didn't come from 'nunnery': Suicide jibe backfires after it is revealed top-court judge's husband killed self," *The National Post*, February 27, 1999.

10. Shawn Ohler, "McClung suffering from 'wounded vanity': judge: 'He owes an apology' " *The National Post*, March 1, 1999.

11. Editorial, "Assaulting the law," *The National Post*, March 1, 1999.

12. Lorne Gunter, "Courtship in monosyllables: Poor manners distract us from the high court's sophistry," *The National Post*, March 1, 1999.

13. Shawn Ohler, "Judge apologizes for 'cruel' attack on senior justice: 'An overwhelming error': Women's groups still want McClung removed from bench," *The National Post*, March 2, 1999.

14. Shawn Ohler, "Groundswell of support rises for embattled McClung: Respected by lawyers: Supporters fear witch hunt against 'gracious' judge." *The National Post*, March 3, 1999.

15. Janice Tibbetts, "Women justices…"

16. Donna Laframboise, "The many meanings of 'no'," *The National Post*, March 3, 1999.

17. Cf. Peter Worthington, "Outrage misplaced in Ewanchuk case; why is a three-time rapist even out on the street?" *The Toronto Sun*, March 16, 1999.

18. George Jonas, "The Canadian Matriarchy's Reign of Terror," *The Toronto Sun*, March 4, 1999.

19. Shawn Ohler, "Women's group turns tables on L'Heureux-Dubé," *The National Post*, March 4, 1999.

20. Edward Greenspan, "Judges have no right to be bullies," *The National Post*, March 2, 1999.

21. Kim Buchanan and Carissima Mathen, Freedom to say 'no' without a crinoline," *The National Post*, March 5, 1999.

22. Christie Blatchford, "Sometimes a massage isn't just a massage," *The National Post*, March 6, 1999.

23. Barbara Amiel, "Feminists, fascists, and other radicals: Claire L'Heureux-Dubé opposes the ideas for which we fought WWII and the Cold War," *The National Post*, March 6, 1999.

24. Kathleen Mahoney, "Feminists, equality, and the law," *The National Post*, March 15, 1999.

25. Alex Kozinski, "An unfair attack on a decent judgment," *The National Post*, March 8, 1999.

26. Brad Evenson, "Judge shuns spotlight in McClung controversy: L'Heureux-Dubé silent: Makes hasty exit after speech to mark Women's Day," *The National Post*, March 9, 1999.

27. John Fraser, "Wait 24 hours before sending a letter to the editor: A lesson learned from Justice McClung," *The National Post*, March 10, 1999.

28. Editorial, "Hardly impartial," *The National Post*, March 10, 1999.

29. Allan McEachern, "Fair hearing," *The National Post*, March 13, 1999.

30. Edward Greenspan, "Judge Kozinski, I beg to differ," *The National Post*, March 11, 1999.

31. According to the Encyclopedia Britannica. "the Mau Mau were a militant African nationalist movement that originated in the 1950s among the Kikuyu people of Kenya. The Mau Mau (origin of the name is uncertain) advocated violent resistance to British domination in Kenya...In October 1952, after a campaign of sabotage and assassination attributed to Mau Mau terrorists, the British Kenya government declared a state of emergency and began four years of military operations against Kikuyu rebels. By the end of 1956, more than 11,000 rebels had been killed in the fighting, along with about 100 Europeans and 2,000 African loyalists. More than 20,000 other Kikuyu were put into detention camps, where intensive efforts were made to convert them to the political views of the government, i.e., to abandon their nationalist aspirations. Despite these government actions, Kikuyu resistance spearheaded the Kenya independence movement, and Jomo Kenyatta, who had been jailed as a Mau Mau leader in 1953, became prime minister of an independent Kenya 10 years later."

32. Alex Kozinski, "Time and place," *The National Post*, March 15, 1999.

33. Marina Jimenez, "Prosecutors want sex offender jailed indefinitely: No- Means-No case: Crown seeks to have Ewanchuk declared dangerous offender," *The National Post*, March 13, 1999.

34. Janice Tibbetts, "Fathers' group to file complaint against high court: All nine justices: Challenge targets 'feminist' slant of Supreme Court," *The National Post*, March 13, 1999.

35. Kerry Powell, "Alberta lawyers want a say in any McClung inquiry: Law firm starts petition," *The National Post*, March 17, 1999.

36. Shawn Ohler, "High court's gender balance leads the nation: Alberta Court of Appeal: Some observers say the split has led to a pronounced schism," *The National Post*, March 19, 1999.

37. Marina Jimenez, "Top Alberta court not as contrary as believed: study," *The National Post*, March 19, 1999.

38. George Jonas, "Some more equal than others? Pshaw!: George Jonas is irked. Despite what defenders of Justice Claire L'Heureux-Dubé argue, Canada has snatched the blindfold from the Goddess of Justice," *The National Post*, March 20, 1999.

39. Marina Jimenez, "L'Heureux-Dubé expected to take a 'lead role': Feminist perspective," *The National Post*, March 24, 1999.

40. Charlie Gillis, "Supreme Court orders man to keep paying ill ex-wife: Decision based on traditional views surprises analysts," *The National Post*, March 26, 1999.

41. Robert Fife and Sheldon Alberts, "PM rejects call for review of judicial rulings: 'We have a good system'," *The National Post*, March 27, 1999.

42. Francine Dubé, "Council rejects complaint against L'Heureux-Dubé," *The National Post*, April 2, 1999.

43. Shawn Ohler, "L'Heureux-Dubé dishonest with judicial body: Women's group," *The National Post*, April 8, 1999.

44. Anne Marie Owens, "Judge L'Heureux-Dubé could be hurt by allegations she lied, scholar says: 'It's a credibility thing': Documents suggest judge was a member of women's federation," *The National Post*, April 9, 1999.

45. Marina Jimenez, "Judges' rules called informal: L'Heureux-Dubé Dispute," *The National Post*, April 10, 1999.

46. Janice Tibbetts, "Chretien's influence could last 'centuries' on Supreme Court," *The National Post*, September 13, 1999. (Emphasis added).

47. Janice Tibbetts and Luiza Chwialkowska, "Louis LeBel appointed to Supreme Court: Surprise choice by PM maintains francophone majority," *The National Post*, December 23, 1999.

48. Luiza Chwialkowska," Revamped bench big on unanimity," *The National Post*, January 22, 2001. (Emphasis added).

49. Editorial, "Supreme bias," *The National Post*, October 25, 1999.

50. Ian Hunter, "Impartiality and the Supreme Court," *The National Post*, November 25, 1999.

51. Ted Morton, "Absence of balance: Public opinion is too divided on gay rights for judges to take sides," *The National Post*, December 8, 1999.

52. Robert Fife, "McClung reprimanded for critical remarks made at L'Heureux-Dubé: No further penalty: Panel says comments inappropriate but not malicious," *The National Post*, May 22, 1999.

CHAPTER FIVE

JUST DESSERTS

"These Chinese street criminals and prostitutes are costing our society a fortune in law enforcement cost and in human tragedy."
—Diane Francis

Perhaps, when corporate media minions distort events involving the brown-skinned people of East Timor or the olive-skinned people of Yugoslavia, it's merely for the political and economic reasons previously indicated. Perhaps there is no racism or bigotry involved. Indeed, perhaps the media are not racist at all, as I'm sure most of them would have us believe. But on the other hand, even some journalists themselves think the media are racist. The relative or entire lack of visible minorities in the newsrooms, let alone at management levels, is one reason to wonder whether this might be the case.

In a revealing and rare newspaper column, *The Globe and Mail's* Michael Valpy contrasted Toronto media portrayal of the January 1999 kidnapping and beating of a wealthy White couple from Rosedale, by two Blacks and one White assailant, with crimes involving Black perpetrators and victims.

Skippy Sigel is a prominent wealthy White lawyer. He and his spouse Lynn were abducted at gunpoint from a $67,000 Mercedes in the well-to-do neighbourhood of Rosedale and held overnight in a dingy 7th-floor public-housing apartment in Regent Park. The Toronto media narrative was about the "almost 12 hours" of horror experienced by the couple. For example, one *Toronto Star* story was headlined, "How kidnap couple survived hell in a 7th-floor hovel."[1] Certainly makes you wonder how some people survive in those hovels every day.

A comparable treatment was afforded to the April, 1994, shooting death of White 23-year-old Georgina (Vivi) Leimonis in the course of a robbery at the *Just Desserts* restaurant in the Annex, another upscale area of Toronto. According to Valpy:

> The media gave the event saturation coverage (*The Toronto Sun*, barometer of crime and underwear events, had the story on its front page for most of two weeks). The media narrative became about bad immigration and deportation policies and cultural problems with child-raising in the Caribbean. In short, Toronto's Black community took a hit.[2]

Valpy suggests we should contrast the *Just Desserts* narrative with the narrative surrounding the sickly murders by Paul Bernardo and Karla Homolka.

> Here the story was not about the cultural problems of a particular racial-ethnic group— European Whites— but about how much of an individual sicko Paul Bernardo is and how, with six billion other people in the world, he could find and marry someone as creepy as himself, Karla Homolka, incidentally (but only incidentally), another White.[3]

Valpy, a rare somewhat-progressive voice at the overwhelmingly corporate and conservative *Globe and Mail*, and in the media generally, notes that just five months after the *Just Desserts* case, a man opened fire on the patrons of the *Whip Burger Menu* in Toronto's west end, killing two people. "The shooter was Black. The victims were Black. *The Whip Burger Menu* is frequented by Blacks. The event fell off the news agenda (as we say) within a couple of days."

Another example involved Christine Ricketts, mother of two young girls and a door-to-door canvasser for *The Toronto Star*, who was strangled in March 1998. Her body was found in the stairwell of a Don Mills high-rise apartment. "The man charged with her death had been released from prison three months earlier after serving time for a violent assault on a prostitute. Ms. Ricketts was Black. Her accused killer is White. Ho-hum," Valpy wrote. Although *The Toronto Star* paid a lot of attention to the story (the murdered woman was, after all one of the paper's carriers), it was a yawner for the rest of the media.

This is one of the ways the media are racist in their coverage: their narrative on criminals and victims. Whites rarely commit crimes, and when they do, they are random and individual acts. On the other hand, Blacks are seldom portrayed as anything other than the perpetrators of crimes, including: the Black drug abuser and drug dealer, the threatening and invasive Black criminal, the Black welfare cheat and queen, and the undeserving Black affirmative action recipient.[4] These Black crimes are said to be deeply rooted in predetermined cultural origins, and/or material conditions for which Blacks are individually and culturally to blame. As two UCLA professors noted after studying television news: "crime is violent and criminals are nonwhite." Perhaps more importantly, the authors found that viewers were so acclimatised to seeing African-American crime suspects on television that even when the suspect's race was unspecified, viewers remembered seeing a Black suspect.[5] Rarely do we see "average" or "normal" Black families. Blacks, and for that matter other minorities, are largely either missing from the media altogether, or receive token representation;[6] they are portrayed as sports figures, criminals, or victims of crimes by others of their 'own kind'; as cute ethnic minorities dressed in cultural garb ranging from warrior tribal outfits to Caribbean parade costumes. Minorities are purveyors and consumers of "ethnic" food. The same holds, of course, for other groups such as Native Canadians, who are mostly depicted as Pow-wow dancers, drunkards, substance abusers, recipients of government largesse, or victims, either of suicide, sexual abuse, or political and economic malfeasance on the part of (naturally) corrupt leaders. As Leslie Joynt aptly put it,

Generally speaking, aboriginal and racial minorities exemplify a 'social problem' as far as the media are concerned. They are described in the context of having problems in need of solutions that expend an inordinate amount of political attention or a disproportionate slice of national resources. In addition, the media are likely to define minorities as villains who 'create problems' by making demands unacceptable to the social, political, or moral order.[7]

As Karim H. Karim points out, "At the height of his athletic career, the sprinter Ben Johnson was portrayed by sportscasters as a national hero; but in the wake of a positive steroid test, the same sources presented him as a deplorable and criminal immigrant from Jamaica."[8]

In 25 years of studying media content, whether news or entertainment, I have observed relatively few exceptions to these unwritten rules. Here's a somewhat more subtle stereotypical example that I came across while writing this chapter, but there are many new examples daily.

BURNING TENT KILLS 37

RIYADH (AP)—A tent caught fire at a pre-wedding party in eastern Saudi Arabia and collapsed on guests, killing 37 women and children and wounding 132 people, newspapers reported yesterday.[9]

This is part of the novelty image of visible minorities in the media, human interest stories about the catastrophes which befall them: they are victims of peculiar disasters, from burning tents to volcanic eruptions and earthquakes. One can just picture the burning tent and the Saudis in their long, flowing robes, victims of their 'quaint' cultural practices such as using tents. In isolation it's not a remarkable story: it is the sum total of the similar representations, whose cumulative effect formulates perspectives. It is instructive to pick up your local newspaper and scan through it, taking note of the way in which visible minorities and those from other cultures are depicted, in stories such as the one above, or in photographs. I have done so with various papers, and have yet to be 'disappointed.'

TOURISTS AND MINERS

A blatant example of media racism pertains to the ink devoted to deaths. Leaving aside the novelty angle in the above story, as we saw in chapter one, hundreds of thousands of brown-skinned Timorese can be slaughtered with barely a blip on the media Richter scale. But just let some alleged Middle Eastern "terrorist" group hold one White American hostage, and this is grounds for a media feeding frenzy. Of course, there is a difference in the nationalities, as well as in the races, in my example. Racism does not preclude ethnocentrism and vice-versa.

In July, 1999, two simultaneous accidental catastrophes provided the opportunity for a paired comparison field experiment. Unlike tightly-controlled laboratory experiments, field experiments leave more variables uncontrolled, in this case nationalities and the nature of the disasters themselves: one was an adventure-seeking tourism disaster, while the other was a work-related mining disaster. But despite the lesser degree of control, field experiments are bona fide methods of academic research, and these disasters happened just a day apart, and (reportedly, initially), involved about the same number of people (18-19). The intrinsic differences might explain away some difference in coverage, but not to the extent that happened.

In the first instance, 19 South African goldminers died from a methane explosion while drilling for the world's largest goldmining company, in the world's deepest mine, on July 29, 1999. The reaction at *The National Post* was to run a 104-word story, two days later, in the *Financial Post* business section, as a "business brief," because of the Anglogold gold mine.

Note that the report is *entirely* based upon what the gold mining company has said about the disaster. No miners or union officials are quoted to get another perspective. There was no follow-up story in *The National Post*: this was the entire extent of its coverage.

The day before this mining disaster, one White South African was among "18 tourists," mostly Australian, who were reported to have died while "canyoning," (an extreme sport described as whitewater rafting with-

> **CARLETONVILLE,** South Africa—A methane gas explosion killed18 miners drilling a rock face at the world's deepest gold mine, owner AngloGold said yesterday. Four search teams were working some 2,700 metres underground at the Mponeng mine looking for a 19th miner still missing after the blast late Thursday. AngloGold, the world's biggest gold miner, said a team of 39 miners had been working on a rock face about 6 p.m. on Thursday when their gas monitors indicated the presence of methane. In line with safety procedures the men started to evacuate the area, but there was an explosion before they were all clear.[10]

out a raft) on the Saxeten River near Interlaken, Switzerland. In response the next day, *The National Post* ran a 750-word story on its front page, detailing the apparent cause of the accident, which was a sudden violent storm causing flash floods, swamping the young people, battering them on the rocks in the river. There was an accompanying Reuters colour photo of rescue workers, a black-and-white AFP photo, and a map. *The Post* also indicated what little was immediately known about the tourists.[11] The story was written by a *National Post* reporter, "with files from Agence-France Presse; Reuters and The Associated Press."

The report carried an interview with a spokesperson for the Bern police; the views of a canyoning expert from Phoenix, Arizona; a manager with *Adventure World*, the tourism company which arranged the trip; local residents' views; a Canadian Department of Foreign Affairs official who was investigating whether there were any Canadians involved; a description of Swiss television and media reports, and a brief word from the investigating Swiss magistrate.

The next day, *The Post* carried a 400-word follow-up article from *The Daily Telegraph* on page three, indicating one more body had been found, interviewing a doctor in the hospital who treated survivors, and quoting the Canadian Embassy which indicated both Canadians on the trip survived.[12]

The day after, *The Post* ran a 550- word story from *The Edmonton Journal*, on page four, interviewing the father of one of the young women, who, while she was on the trip, was not part of the group that was caught in the sudden storm.[13]

The next day, *The Post* ran a 525-word Reuters story, about how the Swiss authorities had launched an investigation into whether to lay charges of criminal negligence against the "four guides" on the outing, who survived. There was more information on nationalities (14 Australians) and the conditions of bodies (relatives were being asked to bring dental records to help with identification).[14] Five days later, *The Post* ran a 130-word story about the announcement by Swiss prosecutors of a formal investigation, by now into the "five guides" who survived the outing, which by now had killed "21 people."[15]

The next day, *The Post* ran a 520-word Reuters article and an AP photo about a memorial service in the resort town of Interlaken Switzerland. "What happened is so tragic. The sadness sits deeper than you'd think," the story quoted a 68-year-old woman as saying.
"Fourteen of the dead were Australians. Two were Swiss and others came from Britain, New Zealand and South Africa," the story reported.[16]

Hence, in sum, *The National Post* ran almost 2500 words in five separate stories about the dead tourists, but just a little over 100 words in one business section story about the miners.

This is *not only* about racism, but it *is* about racism. Of course, the tourists are middle and upper middle class, like most journalists, while the miners are working class, so there is a class element to the bias as well. Ethnocentrism is at play. There are national and geographical elements too, given that there were two Canadians on the trip. (I suspect that if the two women had been willing to grant interviews, there would have been more stories afterwards, as well). But who's to say that the miners didn't have relatives in Canada? No one asked. Additionally, the 14 Australians who died are farther away from Canada than the 19 South African miners, so there is something else happening here besides geographical distance.

One interesting difference is that with Interlaken, the guides, and the weather and even the young extreme-sport adventurers themselves could be blamed for what happened. With Mponeng, it was the world's largest goldmining company, AngloGold, that was to blame. Somehow, none of the media wanted to do this, or even to publicize the news of the miners' deaths.

It wasn't just *The National Post*. A database search turned up five dozen articles about the Interlaken disaster in newspapers across Canada, in *Maclean's* magazine, and a story on CTV. In addition to its news stories, *The Globe and Mail* ran a 1540 word Saturday feature article on why yuppies and thrill seekers take extreme vacations. Why? To "get away from their computers," to tap into "something primal," just "to feel alive," because people "need danger," due to a "need for the wild" arising out of our urban culture, and to "celebrate risk-taking, even if it sometimes leads to death."[17]

Many newspapers carried follow-up articles for several days, as did *The Post*. But when it came to the Mponeng disaster, there were just four short, one-day items, buried well inside the newspapers. Could it be that there was no follow-up news on the mining disaster? Well, as it happens, another miner died in the same mine, during a rock slide, just a couple of days after the explosion, leading union members at the National Union of Miners (NUM) to claim that AngloGold was endangering workers' lives in an unstable mine.[18] This went unreported by the Canadian media, including television.

A week later, on the very day of the memorial service for the 19 miners, three more miners died at another South African gold mine. The government announced that a "specialist team" was investigating the cause of the Mponeng explosion.[19] All this went unreported by the Canadian media. So too did the eventual results of the investigation by the Department of Mineral and Energy Affairs which said the explosion at the Mponeng mine could have been avoided if safety procedures, including the use of gas detectors, had not been ignored. "One of the most disturbing aspects uncovered was a long-standing and pervasive lack of discipline...some protective measures that were in place at the time of the explosion were not adequate, while others were not observed," the government report said.[20]

An assigned reporter could have discovered that 371 mineworkers died in South Africa in 1998, while 6,064 injuries were reported,[21] or that there were an average of more than eight major mining accidents a year in South Africa, over the 14 years up to and including 1998.[22] Since 1984, when the minerals and energy department started keeping computer records, *more than 10,000 miners have been killed* in South African mines.[23]

Immediately after the disaster, the mine union accused Anglogold of gross negligence for not closely monitoring the methane gas levels in the mine, especially since it was a development project.[24] NUM, which represents the majority of South Africa's 25,000 miners, said the disaster should have been avoided. Archie Pilane of NUM said "The explosion occurred 10 minutes after the gas leak was detected. Workers could have been alerted."[25]

Ten months later when 7 miners died following another blast at the Beatrix mine near Welkom, South Africa, NUM held up Mponeng and AngloGold as an example of how, when mining companies were found guilty of negligence, it appeared to have a limited effect on safety measures, accidents and deaths. Noting the similarities between the Mponeng and Beatrix disasters, NUM spokesperson George Molebatsi said, "The Mponeng mine management was found guilty of negligence, but this appears to have had no effect at all." According to Molebatsi, "After each and every accident an inquiry is undertaken and reports are made, but things never go beyond that first step."[26]

In 1995, 104 people were killed at another AngloGold mine, the Vaal Reefs mine near Orkney, west of Johannesburg, when an underground elevator plummeted down the mine.

Mponeng, formerly known as Western Deep Levels South, and its sister mine, Savuka, are the deepest in the world at 3,700 metres. The miners who were killed in the blast were working at a level of 2.7 kilometres or about 1.7 miles below the surface.

According to mine workers, the procedure when extending a new mine shaft is to drill through the virgin rock with long drill bits, searching for pockets of water or methane gas. The driller reportedly struck gas and sent his assistant to warn some approaching miners, about ten minutes before the blast. Despite this, something set off the blast, killing the driller while the assistant survived.

The other miners were approaching from an area about 500 metres away from the driller. Suddenly, the methane ignited in a blast which blew out all of the support structures at that level of the mine. The force of the explosion left many dismembered and identifiable only by their fingerprints. Shift boss Walter Mulovhedzi was one of the first people down the shaft to the scene of the blast.

"There were pieces of the bodies lying around. Hands and legs were ripped off and I couldn't see who was who," a distraught Mulovhedzi said. The men dismembered by the blast were his friends. "I couldn't identify any of them because they were in pieces," he said. Those who survived the blast were crushed by falling rock or suffocated by gas and smoke.[27]

Most of the 19 dead were migrant workers from neighbouring Mozambique, Lesotho and Swaziland, which supply up to 40 percent of the work force in South Africa's gold mines.

Just two weeks prior to the explosion, AngloGold miners, management and owners marched at the British Embassy to protest Britain's auction of 25 tonnes of gold which led to plummeting world bullion prices. The sale, part of a programme announced in May, 1999, to shed more than half the United Kingdom's gold reserves, sent prices tumbling to record lows of $253 an ounce and threatened thousands of mining jobs and economies in Africa.

The very week of the explosion at Mponeng, 4,000 workers went on strike to protest proposed layoffs at the Oryx gold mine. At least six South African mines had already taken steps to fire over 11,000 mineworkers in a country with an unemployment rate of about 30 percent. Another mine, East Rand, was in liquidation with 5,000 miners facing unemployment.[28]

Finding this information is no more difficult than locating and quoting a canyoning expert from Phoenix Arizona. And there is a far more important and interesting story to be written. Not necessarily *instead* of the Interlaken story, but *in addition* to it.

But, Black mine workers in South African don't matter, while White Australian thrill-seekers do.

THE IMMIGRANT FLOOD

Another case study of the way in which the media are racist is in their coverage of so-called "ethnic" immigrants. It's as though we were not all from "ethnic" groups, as though we were not all immigrants, save for the indigenous peoples, all coming here from distant shores, many for one or two generations or less. The 1996 Census found that 5 million Canadians—almost one in five—are, or have been, landed immigrants. Visible minorities, (South Asian, Black, Arab/West Asian, Filipino, Southeast Asian, Latin American, Japanese, Korean and Pacific Islander) not counting the 3 percent of Aboriginal peoples, make up 11 percent of our population.

One of Canada's most visible immigrants is Ng Bing Tse Poy, now known as Adrienne Clarkson, the first visible minority Governor General of Canada. Clarkson was appointed in October, 1999, ironically, during a heated controversy over an alleged "tidal wave" of Chinese refugee boat people arriving in Canada. What's ironic is that Clarkson herself was once a refugee from Hong Kong.

Each year, Canada processes approximately 25,000 claims for refugee status. In the summer of 1999, 590 Chinese refugee claimants arrived on the west coast, in four boatloads. Many of these people crossed the Pacific under deplorable, unsanitary conditions, in the holds of vessels of questionable seaworthiness. Many arrived malnourished and dehydrated. How did the corporate media cover this story? Did the media welcome these refugees from communist China with open arms, tell their tale of woe and bid them speedy assimilation into Canadian society? Did the media betray their economic interests and champion the arrival of the evidently industrious, relatively cheap immigrant labour? No. They chose to promote sensationalist hysteria over the invading "hordes," and to portray the refugees themselves as present or future crooks and prostitutes, and/or as the willing dupes of the crooked smugglers who brought them here.

With few exceptions the media sounded a clarion call about the over-whelming numbers of "illegal aliens" entering, or poised to enter, Canada; they compared, unfavourably, the slightly more humane Canadian immi-gration policies with tougher ones in the U.S. and Australia, and clamoured for the government to toughen up. *The Toronto Star*, which contributed its fair share to the hysteria, summed things up by early October, referring to: "the unprecedented public outcry over this summer's arrival of boatloads of Chinese migrants, a groundswell that has spawned newspaper headlines shrieking such sentiments as: 'Send them home,' [fuelling] pressure for a crackdown on refugee claimants."[29] While *The Star* was intent on poking fun at its admittedly foolish sister tabloids, it too was culpable, and oblivious to the fact that the supposed "public outcry" and "groundswell" were both due to, and largely restricted to, the media.

After weeks of relentlessly promoting their agenda, and as the number of refugee arrivals rose to what the media viewed as precipitous heights, they sponsored public opinion polls, the results of which they distorted in an attempt to show the public was behind them in their racist campaign for tougher immigration laws. This public clamour was then used by the media and their supporters on the right wing, to push the Liberal government to do something about the "crisis." And, while the Chretien government did not immediately change its policies, it did respond to the pressure by jailing the refugees, refusing to release them, and eventually shipping many of them en masse back to China.

Canadian history has documented numerous acts of institutionalized racism against the early Chinese immigrants. In 1875, British Columbia passed the first anti-Chinese laws, denying them the right to vote in provin-cial elections. Other laws further restricted or denied Chinese civil and property rights.

The federal government was just as guilty. The legislative onslaught against the Chinese culminated with Parliament's passage of the infamous Chinese Exclusion Act, which prohibited the entry of all Chinese from 1923 to 1947. This act doomed thousands of Chinese labourers, who toiled in the construction of the Canadian Pacific Railway, to a generation of separation from their wives and children.[30]

The boat people issue was first highlighted in 1986, with the arrival of two lifeboats off the coast of Newfoundland. The lifeboats carried 152 Sri Lankans said to be fleeing oppression in their home country. It later turned out they had come from Germany. The next year, a freighter carrying 174 Sikhs said to be fleeing oppression in India landed in Nova Scotia. They had sailed from Holland. Virtually all claimants from both incidents were allowed to make refugee claims, and most of these reportedly succeeded.[31]

By the time the Chinese refugees began arriving in July, 1999, the media were loaded for bear, as the saying goes. As hostile as the press had been towards the boat people of 1986, A number of events conspired to make the reaction perhaps even more hostile in 1999. One of these was the hijacking of the Canadian press a few years earlier by right wing media mogul Conrad Black, whose views on immigration laws, along with those of his journalist partner Barbara Amiel, are well known.[32] In addition to running the Southam papers and his own Hollinger ones, Black morphed the staid *Financial Post* into the rabidly right-wing *National Post*, giving his views a Toronto presence and additional clout across the country. The Liberal party under Jean Chretien had shifted even further to the right, and the Reform party under Preston Manning had become the official opposition in parliament.

Of course, ever true to its owner's agenda, *The National Post* led the campaign of hysteria, but all of the media were liable to varying degrees. Southam/*Post* columnist Diane Francis, herself an American immigrant to Canada, was suitably apoplectic. With the arrival of the first boat in July, she started off 'relatively' calmly, calling for action over the "convoys of illegal aliens." She wrote: "This week's boat people incident points out that Ottawa must pass emergency legislation, as did New Zealand and Australia in June, to stop convoys of illegal aliens from getting into our society."

For Francis, the refugee hearings were a sham. She knew all about them. "These people are not refugees," she wrote, definitively. "They are opportunists who have agreed to pay handsomely to have someone sneak them in here under false pretenses and without any credentials." At this point she actually restrained herself, merely *speculating* that these people might be criminals or prostitutes or worse. "They may be criminals," she wrote. "They may be prostitutes. They may be dysfunctional, diseased or dangerous."[33]

In August, after another boat had arrived, Francis was raving that, "dozens more stolen boats are being assembled in a staging ground controlled by criminal organizations in Guam and Saipan now that Ottawa has shown complete incompetence at handling the situation." By now, new laws wouldn't suffice: Francis was calling on Ottawa to break the laws: "Ottawa's new immigration minister, Elinor Caplan, must move on this immediately and invoke her authority to collect and deport all those Chinese who have come here so far," she wrote. Francis pulled absurd statistics out of her hat. "Doesn't anyone in Ottawa realize that 40 per cent of Vancouver's crimes are committed by 'refugees' from the Chinese Mainland," she thundered, incredulously. By now she had no problem labelling the refugees as criminals, rather than merely speculating that they might be. "These Chinese street criminals and prostitutes are costing our society a fortune in law enforcement cost and in human tragedy," she wrote.[34]

Other journalists were more calm, even if their goals were similar. Richard Gwyn of *The Toronto Star*, for example, held up the American system as an example for Canadian policy makers to emulate.[35] Gwyn wrote that the American system "is exactly how a refugee system ought to work. Quick deportation of those without serious claims as refugees in order to discourage further attempts to smuggle in illegal migrants." Yet, a news account in his own newspaper that same month detailed the "Bitter asylum," of Chinese refugees "languishing" in top-security U.S. prisons, and a system which greets refugees with water canons to blast their boats away, or with handcuffs and prison garb instead of welfare cheques, health care and living support assistance. "A Cuban whose boat was shot through by a Coast Guard water cannon in June tried to swim the final 150 metres to Florida and freedom. He was greeted with a face full of pepper spray by coast guard officers determined to stop him reaching land,"[36] *The Star* indicated.

Some system to emulate. The U.S. system also suffers from other political biases as well. Tom Walkom notes, for example, that "the U.S. accepted 26 per cent of refugee claimants fleeing a left-wing government in Nicaragua, which Washington opposed. But it accepted only 2.6 per cent of refugees fleeing the right-wing government in El Salvador that Washington backed."[37]

For its part *The Globe and Mail* expounded on how far we have come since our earlier racist days, and then issued a warning that we must not be so generous that we allow others to take advantage. *The Globe* editorialized:

> The spectre of the Komagata Maru is again haunting Canada. In 1914, that sad ship mostly full of potential Sikh immigrants was sent back to India after its passengers spent a hungry, uncomfortable two months unable to disembark in Vancouver...the government of the day, not to mention many people of the day, didn't want Asians of any kind in their version of Canada...The image of the Komagata Maru is again before us as we watch ship after ship full of Chinese migrants steam across the Pacific, enter Canadian waters and then disgorge human cargo on our shores. However, this time our reaction is extraordinarily generous. The migrants are housed, fed Chinese food, given medical care, provided with legal counsel and allowed to plead their rights to stay here as refugees, even though both they and we know they are most likely economic migrants and not political refugees. The irony is that today's boat people threaten to teach us a reverse Komagata Maru lesson. It seems our desire to be fair threatens to turn us into the world's patsies.[38]

In a news report from the CP/Reuters wire services, *The Star* demonstrated how loaded language enters allegedly objective reporting.

GOLD RIVER, B.C. (CP-Reuters)—A decrepit boat loaded with some 190 illegal migrants was seized off the B.C. coast yesterday, as authorities uncovered the third attempt to smuggle human cargo into Canada by sea in just five weeks.[39]

In the span of a single sentence, the refugees are described as "illegal migrants," and then as little more than "human cargo." Even their boat is "decrepit." The fact that it is "the third attempt" at smuggling "in just five weeks," lends to the sense of crisis.

In its news columns, like other media *The Star* was touting legislative change. Australia was still being held up as a "get tough" example as late as November, 1999.

MELBOURNE—Australians have had enough of Chinese boat people sneaking into their country to jump the queues. More than 2,150 people have come by sea so far this year, ten times the figure for 1998. Australian Immigration Minister Philip Ruddock believes the total could yet double in the coming days, with 2,000 migrants poised to slip through Australia's dragnet—After visiting Canada last summer to compare, Ruddock concluded that Australia's hard-line approach makes more sense. "Certainly, on refugee matters, we're a lot tougher," said his senior adviser, Janet Mackin. "Once you hit land, you're virtually assured of refugee status in Canada. Most of the Chinese who arrived [in Australia] by boat have gone back."[40]

As if to prove that criticisms were not racist, *The Star* went to the Chinese community in Vancouver for a negative reaction. "The reaction was very immediate and very negative," Mason Loh, a lawyer and active member of Vancouver's Chinese community told *The Star*. "There were expressions like 'opportunists' and 'queue-jumpers' and 'criminals,'" Loh said.[41] This tactic has long been used by conservative media in the U.S., which like to quote Black Americans who are opposed to affirmative action, conservatives such as Thomas Sowell or Clarence Thomas. John L. Wilks, a Black Republican who served in the Nixon and Ford administrations, described for *The New York Times* in 1991 how these right-wing Black columnists and spokespersons catch on: "They merely say they're conservative, say they're opposed to affirmative action and are immediately picked up by a right-wing White sponsor," Wilks said.[42] Chinese Canadians are just as susceptible to media hype as are Canadians from all other ethnic backgrounds. They are just as susceptible to leading questions, just as prone to having their comments taken out of context, *et cetera*. Here is how Tony Wilden described such "unconscious collusion" or false consciousness in his book, *The Imaginary Canadian*:

> The parasitical ignorance of the dominant in these matters is alone a problem quite serious enough. It becomes even more awesome and dangerous to human wellbeing in its effects when those who are the targets of these real and Imaginary objectifications are so overwhelmed by the insidious power and the daily insistence of these violences that they come unconsciously to believe them to be true. The result will be that they will match their objectification by the Other with an objectification of themselves, by themselves. They will tend to match their stereotyping by the Other with an unconscious collusion in the stereotyped roles laid out for them. They will match the hatred expressed by the representatives of the Other with self-hatred, and with a hatred of others like themselves.[43]

Late in August, the media pounced on support for their oft-repeated allegations that the boat people either were or would become "criminals." *The Star* carried a CP report that "Canada-wide arrest warrants" were issued when 7 of 123 migrants on the first ship "failed to report" to immigration authorities.[44] This segued nicely into the views of Reform leader Preston

Manning, who soon created a splash in the media with his demand that the government jail refugee claimants immediately, give them a quick hearing and deny any right of appeal. Manning took the fairly common conservative view that the courts shouldn't tamper with legislative matters or worry about legal niceties such as due process.[45]

THE POLL AS CUDGEL

The media commissioned a number of polls which they then claimed provided support for their hard line stance against the Chinese refugees, and used them to buttress calls for government legislative action. Even the media which didn't poll accepted the results from the other media, and popular opposition to the refugees became conventional wisdom. For example, on September 1, 1999 *The National Post* published the results of a poll which allegedly showed, "Canadians want refugee laws tightened," which of course just happened to be *The Post*'s position. The first sentence of the story read as follows: "The majority of Canadians believe the country's immigration policy is too lax and should be tightened to deal with the flood of illegal migrants, according to a poll conducted for *The National Post*." *The Post* went on to say the survey showed "that 67% of respondents agree Canada's immigration policy 'doesn't work,' and that it hurts honest migrants and helps smugglers. Only 26% questioned in the COMPAS poll said they think the current system is 'fair and compassionate.' "[46]

The only trouble with this assertion is: the poll results do not support these conclusions, which are based upon shoddy and irresponsible journalism *and* polling. This is readily apparent to anyone who has taken a university level survey methods course.

According to *The National Post*, survey respondents were asked to choose between the following statements, indicating which was closest to their own opinion.

1. "Our policy is fair and compassionate. We only detain boat people who are dangerous. If a court hearing says that a boat person is not a

true refugee and should be sent back, the boat person should be allowed as many legal appeals as necessary even if this takes a long time." Or,

2. "Our policy doesn't work. It hurts honest immigrants, who wait in line and obey the law. It also enriches the crime syndicates who bring boat people here in order to force them into the drug and sex trade. Boat people should be processed quickly, and sent back right away if they are not genuine refugees."

According to *The Post*, "The majority, 67%, agreed with the second statement, while 26% related most to the first."

The second option obviously represents the view taken by the media, and with which they had been bludgeoning audiences for the previous five weeks. But the main problem here is that both questions are "loaded," to such an extent that the answers are meaningless. These are what academic survey researchers refer to as "multiple barrelled" questions, in that they are actually asking numerous questions at the same time. Doing this invalidates the responses, because you do not know which sub-questions respondents actually agree or disagree with. For example, option two above is actually asking respondents to agree with all ten of the following separate and potentially conflicting statements at the same time, and then to choose all of these statements over all of the ones in the first option.

1. Our [immigration] policy doesn't work.

2. Our immigration policy hurts honest immigrants.

3. Honest immigrants wait in line.

4. Honest immigrants obey the law.

5. Our immigration policy enriches the crime syndicates.

6. The crime syndicates bring boat people here.

7. Crime syndicates force refugees into the drug trade.

8. Crime syndicates force refugees into the sex trade.

9. Boat people should be processed quickly.

10. Boat people should be sent back right away if they are not genuine refugees.

Personally, if I were asked these questions at that time I would have agreed with: 2, 3, 4, and 9. I'm uncertain about 1, and 5-8, and disagree with 10. How would you categorize my views? Would you say that I agree or disagree with option 2? The answer is mostly uncertain, with some agreement and less disagreement. And what would you do with me, if you were the interviewer, if I told you that I agreed with some parts in option 1 as well, and disagreed with other parts, and that it made no sense to me to "choose" between the two, as I was being coerced to do?

As indicated above, *The Post* concluded from the survey in its headline and first sentence that: "Canadians want refugee laws tightened," and a majority think "the country's immigration policy is too lax," and "should be tightened to deal with the flood of illegal migrants." In fact, respondents actually were not asked about any of these statements in the question itself, so it is impossible to draw conclusions about them.

Additionally, the biased or loaded wording of the questions themselves weight the answers in a particular direction. For example, option 1 reads in part, "the boat person should be allowed as many legal appeals as necessary even if this takes a long time." Well in fact, this is the law. So, the pollster could have said: "the boat person should be treated fairly under the law," and obviously this would have elicited a very different response, because it is a very different question. If I were designing the question for the *National Post*, and if I wanted to elicit a positive response, I would write the statement as follows: "Refugees fleeing from Communist China should not receive prejudicial treatment under Canadian laws." Most people would probably agree, and then I could happily write a story about how "The majority of Canadians want fair treatment for the Chinese refugees." And my question and story would be far more scientific, valid and accurate than *The National Post* one. But obviously, it wouldn't agree with their agenda.

Their agenda is quite evident even from a cursory glance at the Compas website where they keep some of the results of the polls they conduct for *The National Post*.(Although, curiously, the above results are missing). Here, we can learn about "Faltering Support for Socialised Medicine," with mostly faltering research methodology and analysis, as in "Strong Majority Support for Free Trade" and "Public Concern about the [Jean Chretien] Grand Mère Transactions." These 'survey' results tell us far more about Conrad Black's agenda at *The National Post*, at that time, than they do about public opinion.[47]

This was by no means an isolated incident. Indeed, the Southam newspaper chain was still beating this drum at the end of December 1999, when they published a poll story with the headline: "45% in B.C. poll favoured sending migrants back: A fear that country being held hostage by criminal groups." This story, published in *The Edmonton Journal* but run in the same way across the chain, used another popular media polling technique: 'when the results are split, play up the side you agree with.' The first sentence in the story said, "Almost half of British Columbians believe the boatloads of Chinese migrants who landed on the coast this summer should have been sent straight home." Left unsaid was the fact that despite the hysterical media coverage, the exact same proportion in the survey said the Chinese migrants should: be detained until their refugee hearings (30), be allowed to work until their hearings (12) or be allowed to stay on compassionate grounds (3).[48] So, the headline and first paragraph could equally have said: "45% in B.C. poll favour keeping migrants here," except, of course, this didn't conform to *Mediathink*. Also left unsaid was the fact that due to the small sample size in the poll, the sampling error was such that the proportion of people supporting the refugees could have been as high as 49%, if the population rather than a sample was surveyed, while those wanting to send them back could have been as low as 41%, which means the supposed results are all the more suspect.[49]

ALL'S WELL THAT ENDS WELL

By late in September the federal government was set to appoint a new chief of the refugee board, and the press used the occasion to further push its agenda. Writing in *The Toronto Star*, Allan Thompson summed up the 'problems' the new chief would have to deal with: especially waning "public confidence."

> At a time when public confidence in Canada's refugee system is in the doldrums, the government is poised to appoint a new head of the Immigration and Refugee Board. The next chairperson of the board must grapple with such issues as the influx of boat people demanding refugee status, the backlog of claims before the board and declining public confidence in Canada's system for dealing with refugees.[50]

Of course, public confidence was 'revealed' through distorted media polls, and created through sensational and hysterical media coverage.

The refugee "problem" was predictable, *The Star* reported in late September, if only the government had listened to the author of a 1997 report which said refugees should be held in detention.[51] Over at *The Post*, they reported that the government actually knew what was going to happen, and did nothing, when it could have prevented all of the problems. "Two B.C. Reformers say they are not surprised by secret government documents that indicate Ottawa knew months in advance that a wave of Chinese migrants might be heading to British Columbia,[52] *The Post* said.

Finally, in November, after yet another spate of alarmist reporting, *The Toronto Star* concluded that all's well that ends well, because the refugees did not win. Amazingly, *The Star* reported in a story headlined, "Panic over migrants was unwarranted," that although most of the migrants who arrived in the summer were still in detention, and that "Some have launched hunger strikes to protest their confinement," still, happily, "the first 27 migrants who applied for refugee status have all been turned down by the Immigration and Refugee Board," and a similar fate probably awaited the others.

"Unfortunate as their plight may be, it is proof that Canada's immigration system works—not as efficiently as it should, but fairly." Seemingly oblivious to much of its own reporting on the issue over the previous four months, *The Star* rejoiced that, "the system is not broken," and concluded, sagely, "there is no need to panic. There never was."[53]

For its part, *The National Post* carried on its crusade into 2000 and 2001.

NOTES

1. Dale Anne Freed and Cal Millar, "How kidnap couple survived hell in a 7th-floor hovel," *The Toronto Star*, January 9, 1999.

2. Michael Valpy, "The Black and White of urban crime," *The Globe and Mail*, January 9, 1999.

3. Ibid.

4. Mikal Muharrar, "Media Blackface: 'Racial Profiling' in News Reporting," *EXTRA!*, September/October 1998.

5. Cf. Franklin Gilliam and Shanto Iyengar, "Crime in Black and White: The Violent, Scary World of Local News," *Press/Politics*, Spring, 1996; Martin Gilens, "Race and Poverty in America: Public Misperceptions and the American News Media," *Public Opinion Quarterly*, 1996.

6. Cf. John Miller and Kimberly Prince, "The Imperfect Mirror: Analysis of Minority Pictures and News in Six Canadian Newspapers," Published by the School of Journalism, Ryerson Polytechnic University, 1994.
   http://www.media-awareness.ca/eng/issues/minrep/quick/miller.htm

7. Leslie Joynt, "Too White," *Ryerson Review of Journalism*, Spring, 1995.
   http://www.media-awareness.ca/eng/issues/minrep/resource/articles/white.htm

8. Karim H. Karim, "Constructions, Deconstructions and Reconstructions: Competing Canadian Discourses on Ethnocultural Terminology," *Canadian Journal of Communication*, v18 n2, spring, 1993. Karim cites the article by Hart Cantleton, "How television tracked Ben,"*Content* magazine, November-December 1988, pp. 9-10.

9. "Burning Tent Kills 37," *The Halifax Daily News*, July 31, 1999, p.16.

10. "Gas blast kills 18 South African gold miners," *The National-Post*, July 31, 1999, p. D2.

11. Chris Wattie, "18 adventure tourists die in 'canyoning' accident: 'One corpse after another' drifts into Swiss lake," *The National Post*, July 28, 1999, p.A1.

12. Michael Smith, "Another body found in Swiss gorge: Death toll hits 19," *The National Post*, July 29, 1999, p.A3.

13. Ian Williams, "Alberta pair on tour with canyoners in Alps," *The National Post*, July 30, 1999, p.A4.

14. Suzanne Fenster, "Swiss officials ponder charges in river tragedy: 7 of 19 dead identified,"*The National Post*, July 31, 1999, p.A10.

15. "Guides to be investigated,"*The National Post*, August 5, 1999, p.A15.

16. Alice Ratcliffe, "Swiss town mourns dead in 'canyoning' accident: 5,000 united in grief: Investigators still looking into cause of disaster," *The National Post*, August 6, 1999, p.A16. We also learn that three guides died in the accident.

17. Laszlo Buhasz, "Going to Extremes," *The Globe and Mail*, July 31, 1999.

18. "Another Mponeng mining death," *The Daily Mail and Guardian*, Cape Town, South Africa, August 3, 1999. http://www.mg.co.za/mg/za/archive/99aug/03augam -news.html#mponeng-death

19. African National Congress (ANC) Daily News Briefing, August 12, 1999. http://www.anc.org.za/anc/newsbrief/1999/news0812

20. Quoted in, "Anglogold awaits inquiry into disaster," *The Dispatch Online*, February 3, 2000. http://www.dispatch.co.za/2000/02/03/business/BUS5.HTM

21. Reported in *B2BAfrica* http://she.b2bafrica.com/industry_news/58560.htm

22. "Mine Safety Standards Pay Off," *The Daily Mail and Guardian*, June 14, 2000 http://www.mg.co.za/mg/za/archive/2000jun/14jun-business.html

23. Vivian Warby, "Miners watch in horror as bodies brought out," *The Independent Online*, May 8, 2001. <www.iol.co.za>

24. Simon Nare, "NUM blames Anglogold for negligence," *The Independent Online* www.iol.co.za July 30, 1999.

25. "Accident could have been averted: NUM," *The Independent Online* www.iol.co.za July 30, 1999.

26. "2000 SA miners still face death every day," *The Independent Online*, May 23, 2000.

27. Quoted in Elliot Sylvester, "Could the tragedy have been averted?" *The Independent Online*, www.iol.co.za, July 30, 1999.

28. Darren Schuettler, "Gold bosses picket with 5000 miners," *The Independent Online*, www.iol.co.za, July 17, 1999.

29. Allan Thompson, "WHO IS A REFUGEE?: Ottawa plans tougher detention rules, and braces for opposition," *The Toronto Star*, October 2, 1999.

30. Edward Lee, "Refugee outcry based on racism?" *The Toronto Star*, September 10, 1999.

31. Thomas Walkom, "Shaky sanctuary: This summer's boatloads of Chinese claimants enter a refugee system where good intentions are often overwhelmed by crass politics," *The Toronto Star*, October 2, 1999. As usual, Walkom's writing is a rare exception to the typical corporate media fare.

32. Cf. Maude Barlow and James Winter, *The Big Black Book: The Essential Views of Conrad and Barbara Amiel Black*, Stoddart, Toronto, 1997; and www.blackenvy.com

33. Diane Francis, "Emergency legislation needed now to halt convoys of illegal aliens," *The Province*, July 25, 1999, p.A41.

34. Diane Francis, "Ottawa in full snooze control regarding boat-people problem," *The Province*, August 15, 1999, p.A37.

35. Richard Gwyn, "Canada's generosity an illusion," *The Toronto Star*, September 17, 1999.

36. Robert Russo, "Bitter asylum awaits illegals in the U.S.: Latest migrants from China languish in top-security prison," *The Toronto Star*, September 20, 1999, First Edition.

37. Whittier College political scientist Michael McBride documents the bias in a paper written for the U.N. High Commission for Refugees. Quoted in Thomas Walkom, "Shaky Sanctuary."

38. "Immigration fairness, not immigration folly: The government must turn illegal migrants into lessons for their countrymen," *The Globe and Mail*, September 16, 1999.

39. CP/Reuters, "190 new migrants rescued from rusting Chinese ship: Third human cargo vessel off B.C. coast in danger of sinking," *The Toronto Star*, September 1, 1999.

40. Martin Regg Cohn, "Australia gets tough on Chinese boat people: But number of queue-jumpers just keeps getting bigger and bigger," *The Toronto Star*, November 13, 1999.

41. Daniel Girard, "B.C. turns a cold shoulder to Chinese migrants: Chinese Canadians and larger community united in anger at 'queue-jumpers,'" *The Toronto Star*, October 2, 1999.

42. Quoted in Lionel McPherson, "The Loudest Silence Ever Heard: Black Conservatives in the Media," FAIR, August/September, 1992.
http://www.fair.org/extra/best-of-extra/black-conservatives.html From *The New York Times*, December 22, 1991.

43. Tony Wilden, *The Imaginary Canadian*. Vancouver: Pulp Press, 1980, p. 109. Quoted in Karim H. Karim, "Constructions, Deconstructions, and Reconstructions: Competing Canadian Discourses on Ethnocultural Terminology," *Canadian Journal of Communication*, v18 n2, spring, 1993.

44. CP, "Canada-wide warrants out for 7 Chinese boat people: Freed claimants likely 'scared to death' by plight," *The Toronto Star*, August 26, 1999.

45. Allan Thompson, "Manning wants refugees jailed as they arrive: Calls for ban on appeals, speedy deportations," *The Toronto Star*, September 17, 1999.

46. Stewart Bell, "Canadians want refugee laws tightened: poll: Liberals lose support to Reform, Tories on immigration issue," *The National Post*, September 1, 1999, A9.

47. Cf. www.compas.ca, specifically the polls conducted for *The National Post*, which are listed on that website. I have also critiqued similar problems with the polling and

reporting on polls at *The Globe and Mail*, in Flipside <www.flipside.org> in an article published on June 22, 1999.

48. Adrienne Tanner and Keith Fraser, "45% in B.C. poll favoured sending migrants back: A fear that country being held hostage by criminal groups," *The Edmonton Journal*, December 28, 1999.

49. Whenever exact questions and methods are unreported, as was the case here, it is difficult to properly evaluate a poll. The context of the questions in the survey is a very important factor which is always neglected in reporting. In brief, in the hands of some polling and media companies and reporters, survey research is a highly suspect "science."

50. Allan Thompson, "Ottawa considers new refugee board chief: Successful candidate faces declining public confidence in system," *The Toronto Star*, September 20, 1999.

51. Allan Thompson, "Hold illegals, report urged: 1997 advice could have prevented influx, author says," *The Toronto Star*, September 11, 1999.

52. Keith Fraser and Adrienne Tanner, "B.C. MPs not surprised Ottawa knew early about illegal Chinese: Two Reformers: 'They could have turned them back at an early stage': MP," *The National Post*, December 28, 1999, p.A6.

53. "Panic over migrants was unwarranted," *The Toronto Star*, November 15, 1999.

APPENDIX A

The Independent Women's Forum created the campus project to provide information, guidance, and support for students seeking an alternative to the rigid feminist orthodoxy that is part of today's campus atmosphere. In fact, we are currently running ads in college newspapers nationwide to "Take Back the Campus!" www.iwf.org

April 17, 2001, http://www.iwf.org/news/010417.shtml

TAKE BACK THE CAMPUS

Are you tired of male-bashing and victimology?
Have you had your fill of feminist "Ms./Information?"
Have you been mislead by factually challenged professors?

TAKE THIS TEST:

Campus feminism is a kind of cult: as early as freshman orientation, professors begin spinning theories about how American women are oppressed under "patriarchy." Here is a list of the most common feminist myths. If you believe two or more of these untruths, you may need deprogramming.

THE TEN MOST COMMON FEMINIST MYTHS:

1. *Myth:* One in four women in college has been the victim of rape or attempted rape.

Fact: This mother of all factoids is based on a fallacious feminist study commissioned by Ms. magazine. The researcher, Mary Koss,

171

hand-picked by hard-line feminist Gloria Steinem, acknowledges that 73 percent of the young women she counted as rape victims were not aware they had been raped. Forty-three percent of them were dating their "attacker" again.

Rape is a uniquely horrible crime. That is why we need sober and responsible research. Women will not be helped by hyperbole and hysteria. Truth is no enemy of compassion, and falsehood is no friend.

(Nara Schoenberg and Sam Roe, "The Making of an Epidemic," *Toledo Blade,* October 10, 1993; and Neil Gilbert, "Examining the Facts: Advocacy Research Overstates the Incidence of Date and Acquaintance Rape," *Current Controversies in Family Violence,* eds. Richard Gelles and Donileen Loseke, Newbury Park, CA: Sage Publications, 1993, pp.120-132; Robin Warshaw (with Ms. Foundation) *I Never Called It Rape: The Ms. Report*—With afterward by Mary Koss, New York: Harper Perennial, 1988; Mary Koss, *et al* "The Scope of Rape," *Journal of Consulting and Clinical Psychology,* 1987, Vol.55, pp.162-170; Mary Koss, et al "Stranger and Acquaintance Rape," *Psychology of Women Quarterly,* 1988, Vol.12, pp.1/24. Campus Crime and Security, Washington, D.C.: U.S. Department of Education, 1997. [According to this study, campus police reported 1,310 forcible sex offenses on U.S. campuses in one year. That works out to an average of fewer than one rape per campus.])

2. *Myth:* Women earn 75 cents for every dollar a man earns.

Fact: The 75 cent figure is terribly misleading. This statistic is a snapshot of all current full-time workers. It does not consider relevant factors like length of time in the workplace, education, occupation, and number of hours worked per week. (The experience gap is particularly large between older men and women in the workplace.) When economists do the proper controls, the so-called gender wage gap narrows to the point of vanishing.

(Essential reading: *Women's Figures: An Illustrated Guide to the Economic Progress of Women in America,* by Diana Furchtgott-Roth and Christine Stolba, published by the Independent Women's Forum and the American Enterprise Institute, Washington, D.C. 2000.)

3. *Myth:* 30 percent of emergency room visits by women each year are the result of injuries from domestic violence.

Fact: This incendiary statistic is promoted by gender feminists whose primary goal seems to be to impugn men. Two responsible government studies report that the nationwide figure is closer to one percent. While these studies may have missed some cases of domestic violence, the 30% figure is a wild exaggeration.

(National Center for Health Statistics, National Hospital Ambulatory Medical Care Survey: 1992 Emergency Department Summary, Hyattsville, Maryland, March 1997; and U.S. Bureau of Justice Statistics, Violence-Related Injuries Treated in Hospital Emergency Departments: Washington, D.C., August 1997.)

4. *Myth:* The phrase "rule of thumb" originated in a man's right to beat his wife provided the stick was no wider than his thumb.

Fact: This is an urban legend that is still taken seriously by activist law professors and harassment workshoppers. The Oxford English Dictionary has more than twenty citations for phrase "rule of thumb" (the earliest from 1692), but not a single mention of beatings, sticks, or husbands and wives.

(For a definitive debunking of the hoax see Henry Ansgar Kelly, "Rule of Thumb and the Folklaw of the Husband's Stick," *The Journal of Legal Education*, September 1994.)

5. *Myth:* Women have been shortchanged in medical research.

Fact: The National Institutes of Health and drug companies routinely include women in clinical trials that test for effectiveness of medications. By 1979, over 90% of all NIH-funded trials included women. Beginning in 1985, when the NIH's National Cancer Center began keeping track of specific cancer funding, it has annually spent more money on breast cancer than any other type of cancer. Currently, women represent over 60% of all subjects in NIH-funded clinical trails.

(Essential reading: Cathy Young and Sally Satel, "The Myth of Gender Bias in Medicine," Washington, D.C.: The Women's Freedom Network, 1997.)

6. *Myth:* Girls have been shortchanged in our gender-biased schools.

Fact: No fair-minded person can review the education data and conclude that girls are the have-nots in our schools. Boys are slightly ahead of girls in math and science; girls are dramatically ahead in reading and writing. (The writing skills of 17-year-old boys are at the same level as 14-year- old girls.) Girls get better grades, they have higher aspirations, and they are more likely to go to college.

(See: "Trends in Educational Equity of Girls & Women," Washington, D. C.: U.S. Department of Education, June 2000.)

7. *Myth:* "Our schools are training grounds for sexual harassment: boys are rarely punished, while girls are taught that it is their role to tolerate this humiliating conduct."
(National Organization of Women, "Issue Report: Sexual Harassment," April 1998.)

Fact: "Hostile Hallways," is the best-known study of harassment in grades 8-11. It was commissioned by the American Association of University Women (AAUW) in 1993, and is a favorite of many harassment experts. But this survey revealed that girls are doing almost as much harassing as the boys. According to the study, "85 percent of girls and 76 percent of boys surveyed say they have experienced unwanted and unwelcome sexual behavior that interferes with their lives."

(Four scholars at the University of Michigan did a careful follow-up study of the AAUW data and concluded: "The majority of both genders (53%) described themselves as having been both victim and perpetrator of harassment—that is most students had been harassed and had harassed others." And these researchers draw the right conclusion: "Our results led us to question the simple perpetrator-victim model.")(See: *American Education Research Journal*, Summer 1996.)

8. *Myth:* Girls suffer a dramatic loss of self-esteem during adolescence.

Fact: This myth of the incredible shrinking girls was started by Carol Gilligan, professor of gender studies at the Harvard Graduate School of Education. Gilligan has always enjoyed higher standing among feminist activists and journalists than among academic research psychologists. Scholars who follow the protocols of social science do not accept the reality of an adolescent "crisis" of confidence and "loss of voice." In 1993, American Psychologist reported the new consensus among researchers in adolescent development: "It is now known that the majority of adolescents of both genders successfully negotiate this developmental period without any major psycho- logical or emotional disorder [and] develop a positive sense of personal identity."

(Anne C. Petersen *et al.* "Depression in Adolescence," *American Psychologist,* February 1993; see also, Daniel Offer, and Kimberly Schonert-Reichl, "Debunking the Myths of Adolescence: Findings from Recent Research," *Journal of the American Academy of Child and Adolescent Psychiatry,* November 1992.)

9. *Myth:* Gender is a social construction.

Fact: While environment and socialization do play a significant role in human life, a growing body of research in neuroscience, endocrinology, and psychology over the past 40 years suggests there is a biological basis for many sex differences in aptitudes and preferences. In general, males have better spatial reasoning skills; females better verbal skills. Males are greater risk takers; females are more nurturing.

Of course, this does not mean that women should be prevented from pursuing their goals in any field they choose; what it does suggest is that we should not expect parity in all fields. More women than men will continue to want to stay at home with small children and pursue careers in fields like early childhood education or psychology; men will continue to be over-represented in fields like helicopter mechanics and hydraulic engineering.

Warning: Most gender scholars in our universities have degrees in fields like English or comparative literature—not biology or neuroscience. These self-appointed experts on sexuality are scientifically illiterate. They substitute dogma and propaganda for reasoned scholarship.

(For a review of recent findings on sex differences see a special issue of *The Scientific American* "Men: The Scientific Truth," Fall 2000.)

10. *Myth:* Women's Studies Departments empowered women and gave them a voice in the academy.

Fact: Women's Studies empowered a small group of like-minded careerists. They have created an old-girl network that is far more elitist, narrow and closed than any of the old-boy networks they rail against. Vast numbers of moderate or dissident women scholars have been marginalized, excluded and silenced.

(Essential reading: everything by Camille Paglia; Daphne Patai and Noretta Koertge—*Professing Feminism: Cautionary Tales from the Strange World of Women's Studies*; and Christina Hoff Sommers—*Who Stole Feminism? How Women have Betrayed Women*)

Should you encounter an item of Ms/information in one of your classes, in a textbook, or a women's center "fact" sheet, let us know. We will print it on our campus website, SheThinks.org, correct it with accurate information, and politely inform the source of the mistake. We are a women's group dedicated to restoring reason, common sense and open discussion to the campus.

INDEX

177

COMMON CENTS
Media Portrayal of the Gulf War and Other Events

Objectivity is the theme of these five case studies which deal with how the media covered the Gulf War, the Oka standoff, the Ontario NDP's budget, the Meech Lake Accord and Free Trade.

> Winter provides strong evidence of a corporate tilt in the mass media...it is impossible to dismiss [his] arguments. —*Vancouver Sun*

> Like Chomsky, he enjoys contrasting the "common-sense" interpretation with views from alternative sources. As facts and images clash, we end up with a better grasp of the issues at hand. —*Montréal Gazette*

> Winter's analysis of why the media fail to tell us all, in greater, more useful depth, gives us some basis for hope and humor. —*Peace Magazine*

304 pages, index
Paperback ISBN: 1-895431-24-7 $23.99
Hardcover ISBN: 1-895431-25-5 $52.99

DEMOCRACY'S OXYGEN
How the Corporations Control the News

A book that presents the hard facts that illustrate the complicity between government and corporate media interests as it asks the questions 'who owns newspapers in Canada and what influence have they on content?'

> An invaluable reference tool. Its research is particularly strong in its profiles of the publishing giants. —*Quill & Quire*

> A valuable resource. Winter presents a well-documented case that Black has a definite political agenda, and his acquisition of newspapers the world over is a conscious grab for political power. —*Hour Magazine*

> James Winter has hit on a hot topic. Contains truths which only those in an advanced state of denial could ignore. —*Ottawa Citizen*

> Vividly describes why Conrad Black is probably the most influential opinion-maker in Canada today. A must for all of us concerned about the direction Canada is heading. —*Howard Pawley, former Premier of Manitoba*

294 pages, bibliography, index
Paperback ISBN: 1-55164-060-0 $23.99
Hardcover ISBN: 1-55164-061-9 $52.99

METHOD IS THE MESSAGE
Rethinking McLuhan through Critical Theory
Paul Grosswiler

Examines McLuhan's work in the light of theorists, such as Theodor Adorno, Walter Benjamin, Raymond Williams, James Carey, Jean Baudrillard and Umberto Eco.

In this bold departure from convention, Grosswiler demonstrates the relevance of McLuhan's work for critical thinking about media and cultural change. Will certainly ignite controversy. —*Liss Jeffrey, Executive Producer, The McLuhan Program in Culture and Technology*

McLuhan strikes many media historians as perverse; this book reminds us why he's also so damned interesting. —*John Nerone, Professor of Communications, University of Illinois*

256 pages, bibliography, index
Paperback ISBN: 1-55164-074-0 $24.99
Hardcover ISBN: 1-55164-075-9 $53.99

MANUFACTURING CONSENT
Noam Chomsky and the Media
Mark Achbar, editor

Charts the life of America's most famous dissident, from his boyhood days running his uncle's newsstand in Manhattan to his current role as outspoken social critic. Included are exchanges between Chomsky and his critics, historical and biographical material, filmmakers' notes, a resource guide, more than 270 stills from the film, and, 18 "Philosopher All-Stars" Trading Cards!

The most challenging critic in modern political thought. —*Boston Globe*

One of our real geniuses...an excellent introduction. —*Village Voice*

...challenging, controversial. —*Globe and Mail*

...a rich, rewarding experience, a thoughtful and lucid exploration of the danger that might exist in a controlled media. —Edmonton Journal

...lucid and coherent statement of Chomsky's thesis. —Times of London

264 pages, 270 illustrations, bibliography, index
Paperback ISBN: 1-55164-002-3 $26.99
Hardcover ISBN: 1-55164-003-1 $55.99